Poodle

The
DOG LOVERS'
Guides

Beagle
Boxer
Bulldog
Cavalier King Charles Spaniel
Chihuahua
Cocker Spaniel
Dachshund
French Bulldog
German Shepherd
Golden Retriever
Labrador Retriever
Miniature Schnauzer
Poodle
Pug
Rottweiler
Siberian Husky
Shih Tzu
Yorkshire Terrier

Poodle

By Rebecca Bayliss

Mason Crest
450 Parkway Drive, Suite D
Broomall, PA 19008
www.masoncrest.com

© 2018 by Mason Crest, an imprint of National Highlights, Inc.

Printed and bound in the United States of America.

Series ISBN: 978-1-4222-3848-6
Hardback ISBN: 978-1-4222-3859-2
EBook ISBN: 978-1-4222-7938-0

First printing
1 3 5 7 9 8 6 4 2

Cover photograph by Manon Ringuette/Dreamstime.com.

Library of Congress Cataloging-in-Publication Data is on file with the publisher.

QR Codes disclaimer:

You may gain access to certain third-party content ("Third-Party Sites") by scanning and using the QR Codes that appear in this publication (the "QR Codes"). We do not operate or control in any respect any information, products, or services on such Third-Party Sites linked to by us via the QR Codes included in this publication, and we assume no responsibility for any materials you may access using the QR Codes. Your use of the QR Codes may be subject to terms, limitations, or restrictions set forth in the applicable terms of use or otherwise established by the owners of the Third-Party Sites. Our linking to such Third-Party Sites via the QR Codes does not imply an endorsement or sponsorship of such Third-Party Sites, or the information, products, or services offered on or through the Third-Party Sites, nor does it imply an endorsement or sponsorship of this publication by the owners of such Third-Party Sites.

Contents

Key Icons to Look For

Sidebars: This boxed material within the main text allows readers to build knowledge, gain insights, explore possibilities, and broaden their perspectives by weaving together additional information to provide realistic and holistic perspectives.

Educational Videos: Readers can view videos by scanning our QR codes, providing them with additional educational content to supplement the text. Examples include news coverage, moments in history, speeches, iconic moments, and much more!

Series Glossary of Key Terms: This back-of-the-book glossary contains terminology used throughout this series. Words found here increase the reader's ability to read and comprehend higher-level books and articles in this field.

Chapter 1

Introducing the Poodle

Glamorous, vivacious, clever, and mischievous, the Poodle is a breed with personality plus! Even better, he comes in three sizes—Standard, Miniature, and Toy—so you can pick the perfect Poodle for you.

The Poodle is one of the most adaptable of all dog breeds in terms of his willingness to cooperate with his human family and his physical characteristics. If you want a large, active dog, the Standard is the variety for you. The Miniature will fit into any home, but he is a bundle of energy and will prefer owners that have some get up and go. The Toy is a charming lapdog, but do not be deceived by his tiny stature—he is a real dog and needs to be treated like one.

The Poodle's tightly curled, non-shedding coat is an outstanding feature of the breed. This is a coat that keeps on growing, so regular trips to the groomer are a must. In between trims, though, the coat is very easy to care for.

The other big advantage is that the coat is hypoallergenic, which means it can often be tolerated by people who have allergies to dog hair. However, it is important to test this before getting a Poodle, as some people have an allergic reaction to dander and/or saliva rather than dog hair.

In terms of physical conformation, all three sizes of Poodles are identical. The Poodle is a well-balanced, elegant dog. He is well proportioned and carries himself proudly. His head is long and fine, and the foreface is well chiselled, with fine cheekbones, flat muscles, and tight-fitting lips.

The eyes are dark and portray the Poodle's considerable intelligence, as well as a hint of fire, which is a hallmark of the breed. The neck is long and curved and flows smoothly into the shoulders. The chest is deep and the back is long.

The Poodle comes in a wonderful variety of solid colors, with the eye color and pigmentation complementing the coat color.

Living with a Poodle

The Poodle is a lively, high-spirited dog with plenty of intelligence. His number one priority is to be with the people he loves; this is a dog who bonds very closely with his human family.

The Standard Poodle needs an active life, but generally, the Poodle is ready to fit in with whatever his family wants. He will be happy in town or country, in a mansion or in an apartment, as long is he the center of attention. His motto is, "Include me!"

Originally used as a hunting and retrieving dog, the Poodle—even in the smaller versions—has a strong work ethic. This is a clever dog and, because he is so willing to cooperate with his human family, he makes an outstanding companion.

However, he does need the chance to use his brain, or else he will be forced to invent his own entertainment. A Standard Poodle may become harder to control. Miniature and Toy Poodles are more likely to be demanding, wanting round the clock attention.

The solution is simple: Provide sufficient mental stimulation to keep your Poodle happy and occupied and, in the process, you will establish a close and rewarding relationship with him.

The Poodle tunes in to how his loved ones are feeling, and many owners report a sixth sense, where their dog shows special empathy at times of sadness, depression, or loneliness.

The Poodle can also be quite protective of his family, and may show initial suspicion when strangers approach. However, as soon as he is reassured, he is happy to welcome visitors to his home.

Health and longevity

With a good diet, plenty of appropriate exercise, routine care, and preventive health care, most Poodles will live a long and healthy life. The Standard Poodle will generally reach double figures, while Miniatures and Toys usually make it to their early teens, and some may even exceed this.

The history of the Poodle

When you see a glamorous Poodle in show trim, do not make the mistake of thinking it is an over-the-top fashion statement. It has its roots in the breed's working origins. The name Poodle comes from the German *pudeln*, which means "to splash in water." Poodles worked in the swamps as a water dogs, trained to retrieve fallen birds for hunters.

Their coats were dense and waterproof, which meant they could work in cold temperatures, but it could also impede freedom of movement. For this reason, the coat was trimmed from the hind-quarters to keep the dog from getting bogged down in the water, leaving enough to protect vital areas (such as the heart) against the cold and the dense undergrowth of the hunting grounds.

While the breed has a German name, its origins are not so straight-forward. The breed may have developed from rugged Asian herding dogs captured by the Berbers in North Africa. They traveled from North Africa to Portugal and Spain with the Moors in the eighth century. But that is just one theory.

It may also have developed from the French Barbet, a very old breed of curly-coated water dog. No one knowns for sure.

In France, the dog was named chien canard or caniche, meaning it was a duck hunter. There too, his coat was clipped to help him swim, but was left sufficiently long on the chest to keep him warm in cold water. Some believe that puffs of hair on the tail tip and leg joints were also for protection during hunting, but stronger evidence suggests these pompons came into fashion much later, during the dog's days as a performer.

The Standard Poodle appears in European art and literature as early as the 15th century. Poodles are shown in the works of German artist Albrecht Durer. In the 18th century, Francisco Goya's paintings showed Poodles as favorite pets in Spain. Writers, too, have been inspired by the Poodle. In 1780, Goethe portrayed Mephistopheles as returning to earth as a black Poodle.

Size matters

Looking at early drawings of Poodles, it seems that there has always been variation in size—although certainly, the first hunting Poodles were larger, more akin to Standards. Larger dogs were preferred in Russia, while France and Germany favored smaller dogs.

The variety of size seems to have occurred naturally. The large Standard Poodle and a smaller dog, much like to the Miniature, are depicted in a print as early as 1516. The Toy variety may have come

a little later, but by the late 18th century all three sizes are mentioned in literature.

The French Poodle

The Poodle has always enjoyed a huge following in France, and the French would love to claim the breed as their own. Poodles have been featured in art and literature throughout the centuries, and owning a Poodle was seen as a sign of wealth and status. Louis XIV had a small pet Poodle named Filou, who was featured in the work of several poets and novelists of the time.

From the 18th century onward, Poodles worked as entertainers. Some were in the circus, while others performed tricks on the streets. A large troupe of performing Poodles traveled from France to Britain, where they were celebrated for their amazing feats, which included walking on their hind legs, racing with monkeys as jockeys,

and even tightrope walking!

Standard Poodles were also used in France as guide dogs, guard dogs, military dogs, and to pull wagons. Aristocratic and fashionable women carried Miniature and Toy Poodles as elegant companions. The working water dog clip became accentuated and stylized, and there was a concerted effort by Poodle fanciers to perfect the smaller varieties.

Poodle history

Curls and Cords

The corded Poodle was a refashioning of a 19th century classic poodle coat. The hair on these corded Poodles was never combed out, but allowed to grow. It was continually rolled and twisted, causing longer and longer curls, or cords, to form. Cords hung from the ears, tail, and body. The first Poodle to be crowned a champion in England was a corded dog named Achilles in 1890. He became a legend in his time and was described as standing 23 inches (58 cm) at the shoulder, with cords that hung down 30 inches (76 cm).

Poodles in America

The first Poodle registered with the American Kennel Club was Czar in 1886. He was a black Standard, and was imported by W. Lyman Biddle of Philadelphia. But the breed had actually been in America for some time before that as a working hunter. In his 1891 book American Book of the Dog, W.R. Furness wrote that the Poodle had extraordinary power in the water and "excels all his race in that element, at least, being able to distance the strongest water spaniel and swim round and round a Newfoundland."

The Poodle Club of America was formed in 1896, and in 1931 it was reorganized into the club it is today. In the years in between, the Poodle declined sharply in popularity. Spaniels and retrievers were preferred as hunting dogs, and the Poodle had not yet caught on in America as a companion. The reputation of the Poodle was pretty much that of a fussy little French confection—the ideal gift for one's mistress but not much more.

The Magnificent Duc

The dog who turned all that around was International Champion Duc de la Terrace. He was a huge white Standard with an awe-in-spiring presence and undeniable grace. It's said that anyone who saw him for the first time stopped and stared. He was born and raised in Switzerland by Mme. Emile Warney at La Terrace Kennels. Duc obliterated all competition in European dog shows, winning four Continental championships. He was then brought to England

by Jane Lane, owner of the famous Nunsoe Kennels. He won his English championship, in commanding style, contributed strongly to the Standard Poodle blood lines in England, and had his name changed to Int. Ch. Nunsoe Duc de la Terrace—Nunsoe being Lane's kennel prefix.

Finally, Whitney Blake bought Duc as a gift for her daughter, Mrs. Sherman Hoyt, and the mighty Duc came to America in 1935. *The New Yorker* published a story about his arrival, and a crowd of spectators gathered to view this magnificent animal. He won the Westminster Kennel Club Dog Show that year—the first time a Poodle had ever won it. In all, Duc was shown in the U.S. 18 times and was never defeated.

Again his name was changed, this time to Int. Ch. Nunsoe Duc de la Terrace of Blakeen, to include his owner's famous kennel name. Stories were written about him. The publicity sparked an interest in Poodles that has never waned.

Like the French aristocrats, modern celebrities have plenty of Poodle fanciers, including John Steinbeck, Helen Hayes, Claudette Colbert, Joan Crawford, Duke Ellington, Grace Kelly, Kirk Douglas, Barbara Streisand, Elizabeth Taylor, Jack Lemon, Jackie Kennedy Onassis, Debbie Reynolds, Bob Hope, Lucille Ball, Katharine Hepburn, Walt Disney, Marilyn Monroe, Pablo Picasso, Winston Churchill, Mary Tyler Moore, Maria Menounos, and Rihanna.

Chapter 2

What Should a Poodle Look Like?

Size makes a dog look very different but, in reality, the Standard, Miniature, and Toy Poodle are identical in conformation, coat, color, movement, and temperament.

If you speak to most Poodle owners they will tell you they have the perfect dog, and, of course, they do. Pet owners are looking for the dog who is perfect for what they want. As long as she is loving, has a good temperament, and is easy to live with, she is perfect.

In the world of show dogs, the perfect dog does not and will never exist; every dog has faults. All breeders can do is strive to produce a dog who is fit for the job she was originally bred to, is sound in mind and body, and conforms as closely as possible to the breed standard, which is the written blueprint describing what the breed should look like.

In the show ring, the judge does not compare dog against dog, but each dog against the breed standard. The dog who, in their opinion, comes nearest to the standard, is the winner. However, the breed standard is open to interpretation, which is why the same dog does not win every show.

General appearance and temperament

The Poodle is a well balanced, squarely built, and well proportioned. She moves soundly and has a proud carriage and an air of elegance. She is active and intelligent. The standard says, "Properly clipped in the traditional fashion and carefully groomed, the Poodle has about him an air of distinction and dignity peculiar to himself."

Head and skull

Much of the Poodle's elegance comes from her finely chiseled features and proudly carried head. The skull is moderately rounded with a distinct, though moderate, stop (the step up between the muzzle and the forehead). The muzzle is long, straight, and fine. It is important that the head is in proportion to the size of the dog. Otherwise, the Poodle loses her air of elegance.

Eyes

These are oval and very dark, full of fire and intelligence. The standard says they should be "set far enough apart and positioned to create an alert, intelligent expression." The eyes should not be huge or protruding.

Ears

The ears are set at eye level or just below, and should hang close to the face. The ear leathers are long and wide, and are thickly feathered.

Mouth

The jaws are strong and the teeth should meet in a scissors bite, with the teeth in the upper jaw closely overlapping the teeth in the lower jaw. The chin is defined but should not protrude, and the lips are tight-fitting.

Neck

The neck should be strong and of good length, rising from smoothly muscled shoulders. This allows for the proud carriage of the head, which is a feature of the breed. The skin should be snug at the throat.

Body

The chest is deep and moderately wide, with a well-rounded rib cage, which gives the impression of an agile dog of some substance. The back is short and level along the top, with the exception of a slight hollow just behind the shoulders. The loin (waist) is short, broad, and muscular.

Forequarters

The shoulders are strong and smoothly muscled. The shoulder blade is well angled, so that the head can be properly carried. It is about the same length as the upper foreleg. The forelegs are set in a straight line from the shoulders, and should be straight and parallel when viewed from the front. When viewed from the side the elbow should be directly below the highest point of the shoulder.

Hindquarters

The rear legs are straight and parallel when viewed from the back, with well-developed, muscular thighs. The stifles (knees) are

well bent. The femur and tibia are about equal in length, and the leg from the hock (ankle) to the heel is short and is perpendicular to the ground.

Feet

These are tight, with well-arched toes, and are proportionately small. They are oval, and should turn neither in nor out. The pads are thick and hard. The color of the nails depends on coat color.

Tail

The tail is set high up on the back. It should be as straight as possible, and should not be curled or carried over the back. Traditionally, the Poodle had a docked tail, meaning it was cut to make it shorter. Tail docking is now against the law in most countries, and Poodles are shown with full tails that are carried up. In the United States, though, docking is still allowed, and show dogs' tails are docked "of sufficient length to insure a balanced outline," the standard says.

Movement

Regardless of size, a Poodle on the move is a truly stunning sight. A light, springy action, with plenty of power from the rear, is called for. Movement should appear effortless, and the proud carriage of the head and tail completes the picture.

Coat and color

The coat is the distinguishing feature of the breed. It should be profuse and dense, with short hair producing tight curls. Texture is all-important; the adult coat feels harsh to the touch and will curl within moments of being brushed, unless the dog has been recently bathed.

A Poodle under 12 months may be shown in the Puppy clip. The coat is shaved to an even length all over, except the face, throat, feet and base of the tail are shaved, and there is a pompon on the end of the tail.

Poodles 12 months or over are shown in the English Saddle or Continental clip. In the English Saddle clip, the face, throat, feet, forelegs, and base of the tail are shaved, leaving puffs on the forelegs

Coat, Eye, and Pigment Colors

The Poodle comes in 10 solid colors: apricot, black, blue, brown, cream, gray, red, silver, café au lait (silver beige), and white. Slight variations in shading are permitted, but color combinations are not.

Black, blue, gray: Very dark eyes, black nose, lips, eye rims, and toenails

White, silver, cream: Dark eyes, black nose, lips, eye rims, and toenails

Apricot, red: Dark or dark amber eyes, black or liver nose, lips, eye rims

Brown, café au lait: Dark amber eyes, dark toenails, and liver-colored nose, eye rims, and lips

and a pompon on the end of the tail. The hindquarters are covered with a short blanket of hair except for a curved shaved area on each flank and two shaved bands on each hind leg. The rest of the body is left in full coat.

In the Continental clip, the face, throat, feet, and base of the tail are shaved. The hindquarters are shaved, and pompons are optional on the hips. The legs are shaved, leaving bracelets on the hind legs and puffs on the forelegs. There is a pompon on the end of the tail. The rest of the body is left in full coat.

Some classes may also be shown in the Sporting clip. The face, feet, throat, and base of the tail are shaved, leaving a scissored cap on

the top of the head and a pompon on the end of the tail. The rest of the body and legs are clipped or scissored to follow the outline of the dog leaving a short blanket of coat no longer than one inch (2.5 cm).

Only solid-colored Poodles can be shown, and any combination of colors is a disqualification in the show ring. Parti-colored Poodles (splashes of different colors, as in the photo to the left) are fine as pets, and there's nothing rare or exceptional about them.

Size

The Poodle comes in three size varieties. All are Poodles, and other than size, all should look alike and be judged by the same breed standard.

The Standard Poodle is over 15 inches (38 cm) at the highest point of the shoulders. Most are in the 22- to 27-inch (56 to 69 cm) range. The Miniature Poodle is over 10 inches (25 cm) and up to 15 inches at the shoulders. Most are in the 13- to 15-inch (33 to 38 cm) range. The Toy Poodle is 10 inches or under at the highest point of the shoulders. .

Chapter 3

What Do You Want from Your Poodle?

There are hundreds of dog breeds to choose from, so how can you be sure that the Poodle is the right dog for you? Before you decide to get a Poodle, you need to be 100 percent certain that this is the breed for you.

Companion Dog

The Poodle is an easygoing, fun-loving breed, and the three size varieties mean you can pick the Poodle to suit your home and life-style. Standard, Miniature, and Toy Poodles share the same traits: they are intelligent problem-solvers who need to use their brains. The Poodle is very much a people dog, and needs to be treated as an integral member of the family.

Sports dog

The Poodle is quick-witted and highly intelligent, and he thrives on being given a job to do. This goes for all three varieties. And even though the Toy Poodle may be more limited because of his size, this does not mean his brain power is limited!

The Poodle is as bright as a button and can be trained to compete in many of the canine sports. Poodles of all sizes have reached the highest level in agility and obedience. Poodles are born performers, and with positive and consistent training, they will make their mark in many of the canine disciplines—including sports for retrievers and spaniels. In fact, a small number of Standard Poodles are still used in their traditional working roles as hunters and retrievers.

What does your Poodle want from you?

A dog cannot speak for himself, so we need to view the world from a canine perspective and figure out what a Poodle needs to live a happy, contented, and fulfilling life.

Time and commitment

First of all, a Poodle needs a commitment that you will care for him all his life—guiding him through his puppyhood, enjoying his adulthood, and being there for him in his later years. If all dog owners were prepared to make this pledge, there would be hardly any dogs in rescue.

The Poodle is a home-oriented dog; he loves his own special people and his greatest wish is to be included in everything his family does. If he is excluded, or if he is expected to spend long periods on his own, he will be thoroughly miserable.

He may whine, he may become destructive, or he may get into the habit of barking continuously when he is left alone. This applies to all three varieties, but Toy and Miniature Poodles are more likely to experience separation anxiety. Owners have a tendency to baby these smaller dogs, and inevitably, they suffer when they are expected to spend time alone.

Regardless of the variety, if you have to be away from home for more than four hours at a stretch, you should put off getting a dog until your circumstances change.

Show Dog

The Poodle is one of the most stunning of all show dogs, and if you have the time and patience to learn the art of grooming and presentation, you will find that exhibiting your dog in the show ring is a challenging and rewarding experience.

Bear in mind that keeping a Poodle in the traditional clip that is required in the show ring is a massive undertaking, and it does affect a dog's lifestyle. Weigh up the pros and cons, and seek as much advice as possible before taking this route. Showing can enrich your life—and your dog's life—but you cannot take a casual approach to showing a Poodle.

Serious grooming

The non-shedding Poodle coat is one of the attractions of the breed, but don't be lulled into thinking that these dogs are low-maintenance. The Poodle's coat grows continually, and if it is not properly cared for it will either mat, rather like a sheep's coat, or grow into long, loose spirals that will eventually reach the ground!

The Poodle needs to be clipped regularly—approximately every four to six weeks—and this costs money. You can invest in clippers and learn how to do the job yourself, but this demands time, skill, and commitment. Most owners take their dog to a professional groomer, choosing a trim that will suit their Poodle's lifestyle.

Exercise

Exercise requirements depend on the size of your Poodle. The Standard is a big, active dog, and will need plenty of off-leash exercise. Going down in size, the Miniature requires less exercise, and the Toy's needs are minimal. However, all dogs need the stimulation of being taken to new places where they can run, play, and investigate new scents.

Training

There is a tendency to think big dogs need more training than little dogs. Certainly, a boisterous Standard Poodle who jumps on your lap and demands attention is more of a nuisance than a Toy Poodle. However, all dogs need to be trained, and the reasons for this apply equally to all three varieties.

From an early age, a Poodle (and in fact, every dog) needs to be trained and socialized so that he can find his way in our world. He needs to know what you expect of him, where his boundaries lie, and that in many cases you will be making decisions for him.

If this side of his education is neglected, your Poodle will not always know what you'd like him to do. He may become possessive and guard his place on the sofa, refuse to give up your shoe that he is chewing on, or pull you along on his leash.

There are things you can do to resolve these issues, but it is far better to prevent them in the first place. Training, and especially consistency, are the keys to success.

Poodles are clever dogs, and mental stimulation is a must. In addition to basic training, this might include competing in a sport, more relaxed trick training, or something as simple as going out to lots of different places.

It does not matter what you do, but you need to bear in mind that a bored Poodle will develop his own agenda of attention-seeking behaviors, which could become very challenging.

Other considerations

Now you have decided that a Poodle is the right dog for you, you can narrow your choice so you know exactly what you are looking for.

Size

Size does make a difference in terms of what each variety needs, and this can have an effect on temperament and behavior.

The Standard is obviously a bigger and more powerful dog, and he can be strong-willed and boisterous, particularly during the adolescent phase. With consistent training and handling, he will mature into a loyal and loving companion.

The Miniature and Toy varieties can be excitable—and sometimes very vocal. How much you curb this trait is a matter of personal preference, but in general, a calm dog is a happier dog, so rewarding your dog when he is quiet and not allowing him to become hyped up will probably work well for both of you.

All varieties will get along well with children, although the larger, energetic Standard may be too much for families with small children. For the opposite reason, the Toy may be too small to withstand the rigors of family life and may be better suited to living with adults or a family with older children.

Male or female?

Whether you get a male or female Poodle comes down to personal preference. There may be minor differences in temperament, but all Poodles are individuals, and character will depend more on bloodlines and rearing than on gender.

If you decide on a female, you will need to cope with her seasons, which will start any time from 8 to 16 months on, and occur either twice-yearly or every nine months thereafter. During the three-week period of a season, you will need to keep your bitch away from intact males (males who have not been neutered) to eliminate the risk of an unwanted pregnancy. Some owners also report that females may be a little moody and withdrawn during their seasonal cycle.

Many pet owners decide to spay their female, which puts an end to the seasons, and also has many attendant health benefits. The operation is usually carried out when the dog is about six months old. The best plan is to seek advice from your veterinarian.

An intact male may not cause many problems, although some do have a stronger tendency to mark, including inside the house. However, training will usually put a stop to this. An intact male will also be on the lookout for bitches in season, and this may lead to difficulties, depending on your circumstances.

Neutering (castrating) a male is a relatively simple operation, and there are associated health benefits. It may inhibit overly male behavior, but it will definitely not be a cure for established behavior problems. As for timing, the best plan is seek advice from your vet.

More than one?

Poodles are highly collectible, and you may well decide you want to increase your dog population. Toy and Miniature enthusiasts often find themselves with their very own Poodle tribe! Fortunately, Poodles are sociable dogs and seem to enjoy each other's company. It certainly helps with issues of separation anxiety if you have more than one.

If you decide you want two Poodles, do not make the mistake of getting two pups from the same litter, or even two youngsters who are close in age. The pups will have a great time, but they will bond with each other rather than with you. Housetraining will be a nightmare, and unless you are truly dedicated and are prepared to allocate individual time for each dog, training will be a disaster.

If you want to get a second Poodle, wait at least 18 months, until your first dog is fully trained and grown up, before getting a puppy.

Same-sex pairs and mixed pairs seem to get along equally well. Interestingly, in a mixed pair it is generally the female who takes on the role of top dog. If you opt for a male and a female, you will need to get one or both dogs neutered.

An adult dog

You may decide to skip the puppy phase and get an adult dog instead. It may be harder to track one down, but sometimes a breeder will rehome a female when her breeding career is at an end, so she will enjoy the benefits of getting more individual attention. The breeder may also keep a puppy as a show prospect, but if that potential is not realized, the dog may be better suited to a pet home.

There are advantages to taking on an adult dog, as you know exactly what you are getting. A retired show or breeding dog will be well trained and socialized. The upheaval of changing homes can be quite upsetting, though, so you will need to have plenty of patience during the settling-in period.

Health clearances

As a breed, the Poodle has some inherited disorders in its gene pool. Not every dog will have these disorders, and increasingly, breeders are able to screen for them and avoid breeding affected dogs. When you are looking for a dog, ask the breeder for a full history of the parents, and to see health clearances as well.

The Poodle Club of America recommends that for breeding animals, Toy Poodles should get a DNA test for progressive retinal atrophy, an annual eye exam, and Orthopedic Foundation for Animals (OFA) screenings for patellar luxation. Miniature Poodles should get the same screeninsg as Toys, plus an OFA or PennHip evaluation for hip dysplasia and a DNA test for Miniature Poodle dwarfism. Standard Poodles should get an annual eye exam, evaluation for hip

dysplasia, a heart exam, and screenings for thyroid problems and sebaceous adenitis. It also recommends a DNA test for neonatal encephalopathy with seizures and for von Willebrand's disease.

Rehoming a rescued dog

The Poodle is a popular breed, and although they are easy to live with, some adults find themselves homeless. You may find a Poodle in an all-breed shelter, but it's not easy. Breed clubs run their own rescue groups, and this may be a better option. (The Poodle Club of America has a list of rescue groups on its website.)

It is important to bear in mind that often a dog needs to be rehomed through no fault of his own, mostly when a family's circumstances change. The reasons are various, ranging from illness or death of the original owner to family breakdown, changing jobs, or even the arrival of a new baby.

However, there are cases where a Poodle has not received the training and socialization he needs, and he may have behavioral problems. Typically, a rescue group will be up-front with you about this, and explain how to work with the dog to resolve these issues. Still, you need to think long and hard before you adopt such a dog.

If you decide this is a route you want to go down, try to find out as much as you can about the dog's history, so you know exactly what you are taking on. You need to be aware of his age and health status, his likes and dislikes, plus any behavioral issues that may be relevant. You need to be realistic about what you are capable of achieving, so you can be sure you can give the dog a permanent home.

Regardless of the dog's previous history, you will need to give him plenty of time and be patient with him as he settles into his new home. It may take weeks, or even months before he becomes fully integrated into the family. But if all goes well, you will have the reward of knowing that you have given a Poodle a second chance.

Chapter 4

Finding Your Puppy

Your aim is to find a healthy Poodle puppy who has been reared with the greatest possible care. Where do you begin?

A great place to start is to attend a dog show. You may already have an idea about what size you want, but at a show you will be able to see all three varieties and many of the colors. The classes are divided between males and females and are grouped by age, so you will see puppies from as young as six months, veterans, and everything in between. If you look closely, you will also see there are different types within each of the three varieties. They are all purebred Poodles, but breeders produce dogs with a family likeness, so you can see which type you prefer.

When judging has been completed, talk to the exhibitors and find out more about their dogs. They may not have puppies available, but some will be planning a litter, and you may decide to put your name on a waiting list.

Internet research

The Internet is an excellent resource, but when it comes to finding a puppy, use it with care.

Do go to the websites of both the American Kennel Club (AKC) and the United Kennel Club (UKC), which will give you information about the Poodle as a breed, and what to look for when choosing a puppy. You will also find contact details for breed clubs.

Both sites may have lists of breeders, and you can look for breeders of merit from the AKC, which indicates that a code of conduct has been followed.

Do go to the sites of the national and local breed clubs. On breed club websites you will find lots of useful information that will help you to care for your Poodle. There may be contact details of breeders in your area. Some websites also have a list of breeders who have

puppies available. The advantage of going through a breed club is that members will follow a code of ethics, and this will give you some guarantees regarding the puppy's parents and health checks.

If you are planning to show your Poodle, you will need to find a breeder that specializes in show lines and has a reputation for producing top-quality dogs.

Remember that health and temperament are top priorities, so do not overlook these considerations when you are researching pedigrees.

Do not look at puppies for sale. There are legitimate Poodle breeders with their own websites, and they may, occasionally advertise a litter, although in most cases reputable breeders have waiting lists for their puppies before they are even born.

The danger comes from unscrupulous breeders who produce puppies purely for profit, with no thought for the health of the dogs they breed and no care given to rearing the litter.

Photos of puppies are hard to resist, but never make a decision based purely on an online advertisement. You need to find out who the breeder is, and have the opportunity to visit their premises and inspect the litter before making a decision.

Responsible breeders

Responsible breeders raise their puppies at home and underfoot. They have one or, at the most, two litters at a time. They carefully study the pedigrees of the male and female before they arrange any breeding, with an eye toward breeding the healthiest, most temperamentally sound dogs. Responsible breeders belong to a breed club and are involved in their breed.

Responsible breeders register their puppies with a well-established registry such as the AKC or the UKC. (Registration with a well-established kennel club is a guarantee that your Poodle is truly a Poodle, but it is not a guarantee of good health or temperament.) They are able to hand over registration documents at the time of sale. Their breeding dogs are permanently identified by microchip or DNA. They screen them for hereditary health problems, and can tell you exactly which screening tests their dogs have had and what the results were.

You should be able to meet the mother and see where the puppies are kept. Everything should look and smell clean and healthy. The mother should be a well-socialized dog. She may be a little protective of her babies, but she should act like a typical Poodle.

Responsible breeders socialize all their puppies in a home environment. They provide written advice on feeding, ongoing training, socialization, parasite control, and vaccinations. They are available for phone calls after you buy their puppies, and will take a dog back at any time. They have a written contract of sale for each puppy that conforms to your state's laws.

Questions, questions, questions

When you find a responsible breeder with puppies available, you will have lots of questions to ask. These should include:

- Where have the puppies been reared?
- How many are in the litter? What is the split of males and females?
- How many have already been spoken for? The breeder will probably be keeping a puppy to show or for breeding, and there may be other people on a waiting list.
- Can I see the mother with her puppies?
- What age are the puppies now?
- When will they be ready to go to their new homes?

Bear in mind that puppies need to be with their mother and siblings until they are a minimum of 10 weeks of age. Otherwise they miss out on vital learning and communication skills, which will have a detrimental effect on them for the rest of their lives. At 10 weeks Toy Poodles are also a little bigger and more able to cope with the upheaval of leaving the litter and their familiar surroundings.

The breeder should also have lots and lots of questions for you. Don't be offended! They take seriously their responsibility for every puppy they produce, and that's a good thing.

You will be asked some or all of the following questions:

- What is your previous experience with dogs?
- Do you already have other dogs at home?

- What is your home set-up?
- Is there somebody at home most of the time?
- Do you have children or grandchildren? What are their ages?
- Do you want to show your Poodle?
- Do you plan to compete with your Poodle in a canine sport?

The breeder is not being intrusive; they need to understand the type of home you will provide so they can make the right match. The breeder is doing it for both the dog's benefit and also for yours.

Steer clear of a breeder who does not ask you questions. He or she may be more interested in making money from the puppies than ensuring that they go to good homes. They may also have taken other short cuts, which may prove disastrous, and very expensive, in terms of vet bills and heartache.

Puppy watching

A litter of Poodle puppies is totally irresistible. Rushing up to greet you, this band of mop-headed ragamuffins—so different from the glamorous full-coated adults—all seem to say, "Take me home!" However, you must try to put your feelings aside so that you can make an informed choice.

You need to be 100 percent confident that the parents are healthy, and the puppies have been reared with love and care, before making a commitment to buy.

Viewing a litter

It is a good idea to have a mental checklist of what to look for when you visit a breeder. You want to see:

- A clean, hygienic environment.
- Puppies who are outgoing, friendly, and eager to meet you.
- A sweet mother who is ready to show off her puppies.
- Pups who are well-fleshed-out but not pot-bellied (which could be an indication of worms).
- Bright eyes, with no sign of soreness or discharge.
- Clean ears that smell fresh.
- No discharge from the eyes or nose.
- Clean rear ends.
- Lively pups who are keen to play.

It is important that you see the mother with her puppies, as this will give you a good idea of the temperament they are likely to inherit. It is also helpful if you can see other close relatives, so you can assess the type and temperament that the breeder produces.

In most cases, you will not be able to see the father (sire) as most breeders will travel some distance to find a stud dog

who is not too close to their own bloodlines and complements their bitch. However, you should be able to see photos of him and examine his pedigree, which will help you to make an informed decision.

Companion puppy

In most cases, you will be wanting a Poodle purely as a companion, and in this matter, your choice should be guided by the breeder. It is tempting to go for the pup who comes up to you first, or the one who makes you laugh as she chases her siblings.

But the breeder will have spent hours and hours watching the puppies as they have developed from newborns. They have an in-depth knowledge of how the puppies interact with each other, with other dogs in the family, how they relate to people, and how they cope with new experiences. This is invaluable information when making the right match. The breeder will also take into account your family set-up and lifestyle and will help you to pick the most suitable puppy.

Show puppy

Do you have ambitions to exhibit your Poodle in the show ring? If so, you need to make your intentions clear to the breeder so you can select a puppy who has the potential to be successful in the ring.

The aim is to find a Poodle who will, when full grown, conform closely to the Breed Standard. This is no easy matter when a puppy is only eight to ten weeks old, so it is worth recruiting an expert to evaluate the litter. The breeder will also help you make a choice, they will only want their best-quality dogs to be exhibited at shows.

Sports dog

All Poodles can be trained, but some may have a greater aptitude, depending on the temperament they have inherited. There are a few basic tests you can carry out which will help you assess working potential. These tests need to be carried out on each individual puppy.

Get hold of a toy—or even a crumpled-up piece of paper—and throw it. A pup with a strong instinct to retrieve will run out and bring it back to you. Walk away from the pup and see if she follows. A working dog needs a degree of independence, but she also needs to be people oriented.

Drop an object, such as a pot lid, when the puppy's attention is focused elsewhere. She should react to the noise but recover quickly. This will indicate that she is not too sound sensitive.

Remember, temperament and health should always be the major considerations, as the time spent working a dog during her lifetime is very small compared to the time spent living at home as a member of your family

Chapter 5

A Poodle-
Friendly Home

I t may seem like forever before your puppy is ready to leave the
breeder and come home with you. But you can fill the time by getting your home ready and buying the equipment you will need.
These preparations apply to a new puppy but, in reality, they are the
way you will create an environment that is safe and secure for your
Poodle throughout his life.

At home

Nothing is safe when a puppy is about—and this is certainly true
of the inquisitive Poodle. Everything is new and exciting for a young
puppy. It all needs thorough investigation—and this usually means
testing things with mouth and teeth. One thing is certain—an unsupervised Poodle puppy cannot be trusted! Remember, it is not only
your prized possessions that are under threat; so is your puppy, who
can accidentally hurt himself quite seriously.

Look around and ask yourself what mischief a puppy could get

up to and what he could chew. Electric cords are prime candidates, so these should be safely secured where a puppy cannot reach them. Try running exposed cords and cables through PVC pipe to keep little teeth away. Anything breakable, such as glass or china, is very dangerous—once broken by a wagging tail, a puppy could step on sharp pieces or even swallow them. Houseplants also need to be out of reach, as, even if they are not poisonous, they will very likely upset a puppy's tummy.

You will need to make sure all cupboards and storage units cannot be opened—or broken into. This applies particularly in the kitchen and bathroom, where you may store cleaning materials and other substances that are toxic to dogs.

If you have stairs, it would be wise to declare upstairs off-limits. Negotiating stairs can be hazardous, particularly for a tiny Toy Poodle. The best way to do this is to use a baby gate—but make sure your puppy can't squeeze through it, or under it, when he is very small.

In the yard

It is unusual for a Poodle to stray far from his people, but you need to check that your yard is safe and secure. The height of fencing required depends on the size of your Poodle. A Standard can jump over, and a Toy can wriggle under or squeeze through tiny gaps. To be on the safe side, fencing should be a minimum height of 5 feet (1.5 m), and should be checked regularly. If you have a gate leading out of the yard, it should fasten securely.

Poodles are enthusiastic diggers, so you may decide to fence off part of the garden, so your prized plants are not ruined. Find out if your garden contains plants that are poisonous to dogs. There is not enough room to list them all here, but you can find a full list at www.aspca.org/pet-care/animal-poison-control/toxic-and-non-toxic-plants.

Swimming pools and ponds should be covered, as most puppies are fearless and, although it is easy for a puppy to take the plunge, it is virtually impossible for him to get out unaided.

You will also need to designate a toileting area. This will help with the housetraining process, and it will also make cleaning up easier.

House rules

Before your puppy comes home, hold a family conference to decide on the house rules. You need to decide which rooms your puppy will have access to, and establish whether he is to be allowed on the furniture. The Toy Poodle sees himself as a lapdog and would be pretty insulted if he was not allowed on the sofa—but you may not feel like being so lenient with a Standard! It is all a matter of figuring out what is right for you and your family.

The most important thing is to be consistent, so that your Poodle understands the rules. He will be very confused if one member of the family allows him on the sofa for a cuddle and someone else tells him off when he tries to do the same thing.

Going shopping

There are some essential items you will need for your Poodle. If you choose wisely, much of it will last for many years to come.

Indoor crate

Rearing a puppy is so much easier if you invest in an indoor crate. It provides a safe haven for your puppy at night, when you have to go out during the day, and at other times when you cannot supervise him. A puppy needs a base where he feels safe and secure, and where he can rest undisturbed. An indoor crate provides the perfect den, and many adult dogs continue to use them throughout their lives. If you have a Standard Poodle, make sure you buy a crate that will be big enough to accommodate him when he is fully grown.

You will also need to think about where you are going to put the crate. The kitchen is often the most suitable place, as this is the hub

of family life. Find a snug corner where the puppy can rest when he wants to, but where he can also see what is going on around him and still be with the family.

Playpen

This is not essential, but playpens are becoming increasingly popular with puppy owners. You can set up the playpen indoors or out, line it with bedding, and equip it with toys so your puppy has a safe area to play—and cannot get into mischief.

Beds and bedding

The crate and playpen will need to be lined with bedding. The best type is synthetic fleece which is warm and cozy. It is also machine washable and easy to dry. An added advantage is that moisture soaks through the bedding, so when your puppy is going through the housetraining process there is no risk of him being left in a wet bed.

If you have purchased a crate, you may not feel the need to buy an extra bed. However, the Poodle enjoys his creature comforts and he will certainly appreciate additional sleeping quarters. There is an amazing array of dog beds to chose from—sofas, bean bags, cushions, baskets, igloos, mini-four posters—so you can take your pick! You do need to bear in mind that some beds prove irresistible as far as chewing is concerned, so put off making a major investment until your Poodle has outgrown the destructive puppy phase.

Collar and leash

You may think that it is not worth buying a collar for the first few weeks, but the sooner your pup gets used to it, the better. A nylon lightweight collar is fine, as most puppies will accept it without making a fuss. Be careful when you are fitting the collar that it is not too tight and not too loose. A good guideline is to make sure you can fit two fingers under the collar.

There are plenty of leashes to choose from. Choose a material, such as leather or soft nylon, that is kind to your hands and also has a secure trigger clip.

If you have a Toy Poodle, make sure the collar and leash are small

and lightweight, so they do not weigh down his little neck. Some people prefer to walk Toy dogs on a harness and leash.

An extending leash can be useful to give your Poodle limited freedom when it is not safe or permitted to allow him off-leash. However, you should never use it when walking on the street. If your Poodle pulls unexpectedly and the leash extends more than you intend, it could have disastrous consequences.

Grooming a Toy Poodle

ID

Your Poodle needs to wear some form of ID when he is out in public. This can be in the form of a tag engraved with your contact details and attached to the collar. When your Poodle is full-grown, you can buy an embroidered collar with your contact details, which eliminates the danger of the tag falling off.

You may also wish to consider a permanent form of ID. Increasingly, breeders are getting puppies microchipped before they go to their new homes. A microchip is the size of a grain of rice. It is injected under the skin, usually between the shoulder blades, with a special needle.

Each chip has its own unique identification number that can only be read by a special scanner. That ID number is then registered on a national database with your name and details, so if your dog is lost, any veterinarian or shelter where he is scanned can contact you. If your puppy has not been microchipped, you can ask your vet to do it, maybe when he goes in for his vaccinations.

Bowls

Your Poodle will need two bowls; one for food, and one for fresh drinking water, which should always be readily available. A stainless steel bowl is a good choice for a food bowl. Plastic bowls will almost certainly be chewed, and there is a danger that bacteria can collect in the small cracks that may appear. You can get for a second stainless steel bowl for drinking water, or you may prefer a heavier ceramic bowl, which will not be knocked over so easily.

Food

The breeder will let you know what your puppy is eating and should provide a full diet sheet to guide you through the first six months of your puppy's feeding regime—how much he is eating per meal, how many meals per day, when to increase the amounts per meal, and when to reduce the meals per day.

The breeder may provide you with some food when you pick up your puppy, but it is worth making inquiries in advance about the availability of the brand that is recommended.

Grooming gear

If you are planning to use a professional groomer, you will only need a few basic pieces of equipment to keep your Poodle's coat in good order between trips to the groomer.

- Slicker brush
- Wide-toothed metal comb
- Nail clippers: the guillotine type are easy to use
- Toothbrush and toothpaste: choose between a long-handled toothbrush or a finger brush, whichever you find easiest; there are flavored canine toothpastes on the market that your dog will enjoy

Toys

Poodles love their toys—and not just puppies! But before you get carried away buying a vast range of toys to keep your puppy entertained, you need to think about which are the safest. Plastic toys can be shredded, cuddly toys can be chewed, and toys where the squeaker can be removed should be avoided at all costs. If your Poodle ingests part of a toy, it could well result in an internal blockage, and the results of this are often fatal.

All toys should be checked regularly for wear and tear, and do not leave your puppy with a toy when he is not being supervised. The exception to this is if you buy a hard rubber Kong-type toy, which can be stuffed with food. This is 100 percent safe and will give your Poodle something to keep him busy when you must leave him home alone.

Finding a veterinarian

Do this before you bring your dog home, so you have a vet to call if there is a problem. Visit some of the vets in your area, and speak to other pet owners to find out who they recommend. It is as important to find a good vet as it is to find a good doctor for yourself. You need to find someone with whom you can build a good rapport and have complete faith in. Word of mouth is really the best recommendation.

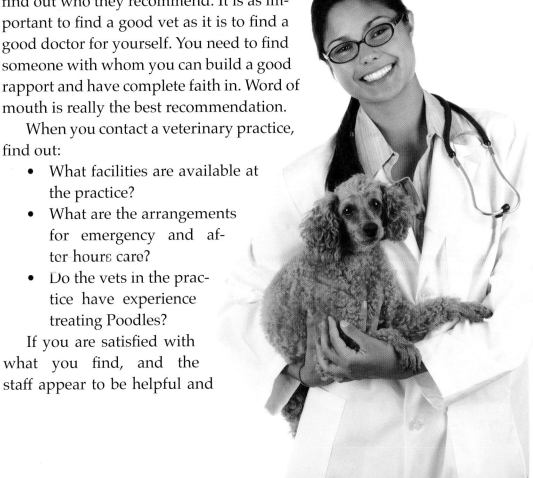

When you contact a veterinary practice, find out:

- What facilities are available at the practice?
- What are the arrangements for emergency and after hours care?
- Do the vets in the practice have experience treating Poodles?

If you are satisfied with what you find, and the staff appear to be helpful and friendly, book an appointment so your puppy can have a health check a couple of days after you bring him home. The vet will need to see the vaccination record and will record all the details both for you and the dog. He or she will discuss with you feeding, worming, parasite treatments, and probably microchipping, at the first visit.

Settling in

When you first arrive home with your puppy, be careful not to overwhelm him. You and your family are hugely excited, but the puppy is in a completely unfamiliar environment with new sounds, smells, and sights. This is a daunting experience, even for the boldest of pups.

Some puppies are very confident, wanting to play right away and quickly making friends; others need a little longer. Keep a close eye on your Poodle's body language and reactions so you can proceed at a pace he is comfortable with.

First, let him explore a little bit outside. He will probably need to relieve himself after the trip home, so take him to the designated toileting area and, when he performs, give him plenty of praise.

When you take your puppy indoors, let him investigate again. Show him his crate, and encourage him to enter by throwing in a treat. Let him sniff, and allow him to go in and out as he wants. Later on, when he is tired, you can put him in the crate while you stay in the room. This way, he will learn to settle and will not think he is being abandoned.

It is a good idea to feed your puppy in his crate, at least to begin with, as this helps to build up a positive association. It will not be long before your Poodle sees his crate as his own special den and will go there on his own. Some owners place a blanket over the crate, covering the back and sides, so that it is even more cozy and den-like.

Meeting the family

Resist the temptation to invite friends and neighbors to come and meet the new arrival. Your puppy needs to focus on getting to know his new family for the first few days. Try not to swamp your Poodle with too much attention—he needs a chance to explore and find his own way. There will be plenty of time for cuddles later on!

If you have children in the family, you need to keep everything as calm as possible. The Poodle will make an outstanding family companion, but a sense of mutual respect must be established. A Toy Poodle is not the best choice for small children but older children also need to learn how to behave with the new addition to the family. He may be called a Toy Poodle but he is definitely not a toy! He needs to be treated like a proper dog, which means:

- He should not be picked up and carried around
- He should not be teased
- He should be left in peace when he goes to his bed or crate
- He should not be disturbed when he is eating

Bear in mind, it is easy for a puppy to become over-excited by raised voices, or by children running around and behaving unpredictably, and this can easily lead to mouthing and nipping.

The best plan is to get the children to sit on the floor and give them each a treat. Each child can then call the puppy, pet him, and offer the treat. This way, the puppy interacts with each child calmly and sensibly to get his treat.

If he tries to nip or mouth, make sure there is a toy ready nearby, so his attention can be diverted to something he is allowed to bite. If you do this consistently, he will learn to inhibit his desire to mouth when he is interacting with people.

Right from the start, impose a rule that the children are not allowed to pick up or carry the puppy. They can cuddle him when they are sitting on the floor. This may sound a little severe, but a wriggly puppy can be dropped in an instant, with possible severe consequences.

Involve all family members with your puppy's day-to-day care. This will develop his bond with the whole family, as opposed to just one person. Encourage the children to train and reward the puppy, so he learns to follow commands from everyone in the family.

The resident dog

Poodles are sociable dogs, and it is rare to have problems when introducing a new puppy to the resident animal family. However, it is best to take nothing for granted and to supervise early interactions.

In an ideal scenario, introduce your resident dog to the newcomer at the breeder's home. This works well because the puppy feels secure and the adult dog does not feel threatened. But if this is not possible, allow your dog to smell the puppy's bedding (bedding supplied by the breeder is fine) before they actually meet, so he familiarizes himself with the puppy's scent.

Outdoors is the best place for introducing the puppy, since the adult will regard it as neutral territory. He will probably take a great interest in the puppy and sniff him all over. Most puppies are naturally submissive in this situation, and your pup may lick the other dog's mouth or roll over on to his back. Try not to interfere, as this is the natural way dogs get to know each other.

You will only need to intervene if the older dog is too boisterous, and alarms the puppy. In this case, it is a good idea to put the adult on his leash so you have some measure of control.

It rarely takes long for an adult to accept a puppy, since he does not constitute a threat. This will be underlined if you make a big fuss over the older dog, so he has no reason to feel jealous.

Feline friends

The Poodle does not have a particularly strong prey drive, although the Standard is more inclined to chase a cat than the Toy or Miniature varieties. Harmonious relations can be established with the family cat if you work hard at early interactions. You will need to progress step by step, making sure the pair are never left alone together until they have learned to ignore each other.

If your Poodle seems very focused on the cat, keep the dog on a leash for the first couple of meetings so your puppy has a chance to

make his acquaintance in a controlled situation. Keep calling your puppy to you and rewarding him so that he does not get obsessed with cat watching. When you allow your puppy to go free, make sure the cat has an easy escape route, just in case the dog tries to chase.

This is an ongoing process, but all the time your Poodle is learning that he is rewarded for ignoring the cat. In time, the novelty will wear off and the pair will live in peace—who knows, they may even become the best of friends!

The most important thing you can do is make sure your cat has plenty of elevated spots in every room, well out of the puppy's reach, to which she can retreat. Feed her up high, as well, so she will not be bothered. And if the puppy is showing too much interest in her litter box, put it in a room that is blocked with a baby gate, so kitty can go over but the puppy can't get in.

Feeding

The breeder will generally provide enough food for the first few days, so your puppy does not have to cope with a change in diet—and possible digestive upset—along with all the stress of moving to a new home.

Some puppies eat up their food from the very first meal; others are more concerned about their new surroundings and are too distracted to eat. Do not worry if your puppy seems uninterested in his food for the first day or so. Give him 10 minutes to eat what he wants and then remove the leftovers and give him fresh food at the next meal.

Obviously, if you have any concerns about your puppy in the first few days, seek advice from your veterinarian.

If your Poodle seems to lose interest in his food, try feeding him in his crate where he can eat in peace and will not be so distracted.

It is also advisable to work on your Poodle's food manners, so he never feels

Rescued Dogs

Settling in an adult dog is very similar to a puppy, in as much as you will need to make the same preparations for his homecoming. As with a puppy, an adult dog will need you to be consistent, so start as you mean to go on.

There is often an initial honeymoon period when you bring a rescued dog home, where he will be on his best behavior for the first few weeks. It is after these first couple of weeks that the true nature of the dog will show, so be prepared for subtle changes in his behavior.

It may be advisable to register with a reputable training club, so you can seek advice on any training or behavior issues at an early stage.

Above all, remember that a rescued dog ceases to be a rescued dog the moment he enters his forever home with you.

threatened when he is eating and does not become protective of his food bowl. You can do this by giving him half his meal, and then dropping food around his bowl. This will prevent him from guarding his bowl and, at the same time, he will see your presence in a positive light.

You can also call him away from the bowl and reward him with some food—maybe something extra special—which he can take from your hand. Start doing this as soon as your puppy arrives in his new home, and continue working on it throughout his life.

The first night

Your puppy will have spent his entire life so far with his mother or curled up with his siblings. He is then taken from everything he knows as familiar, lavished with attention by his new family—and then comes bedtime when he is left all alone. It is little wonder that he feels abandoned!

The best plan is to establish a nighttime routine, and then stick to it so that your puppy knows what is expected of him. Take your puppy outside to relieve himself, and then settle him in his crate. Some people leave a low light on for the puppy at night for the first week, others have tried soft music as company or a ticking clock. A covered hot-water bottle filled with warm water can also be a comfort. Like people, puppies are all individuals and what works for one, does not necessarily work for another, so it is a matter of trial and error.

Be very positive when you leave your puppy on his own. Do not linger or keep returning; this will make the situation more difficult.

It is inevitable that he will protest to begin with, but if you stick to your routine, he will accept that he gets left at night—but you always return in the morning.

Housetraining

This is an aspect of training that first-time owners dread, but if you start as you mean to go on, it will not be long before your Poodle understands what is required. The key to successful housetraining is vigilance and consistency. If you establish a routine and you stick to it, your puppy will understand what is required.

Equally, you must be there to supervise him at all times—except when he is safely tucked away in his crate. It is when a puppy is left to wander from room to room that accidents are most likely to happen.

You will have allocated a toileting area in your yard or somewhere else outdoors when preparing for your puppy's homecoming.

Take your puppy to this area every time he needs to relieve himself so he builds up an association and knows why you have brought him outside.

Establish a routine and make sure you take your puppy out at the following times:

- First thing in the morning
- After mealtimes
- When he wakes up
- After a play session
- Last thing at night

A puppy should be taken out to relieve himself every two hours as an absolute minimum. If you can manage an hourly trip out, so much the better. The more often your puppy gets it right, the quicker he will learn to be clean in the house. It helps if you use a verbal cue, such as "busy," when your pup is performing, and in time, this will trigger the desired response.

Do not be tempted to put

Tips on housetraining a puppy.

your puppy out on the doorstep to the backyard in the hope that he will toilet on his own. Most pups simply sit there, waiting to get back inside the house! No matter how bad the weather is, accompany your puppy and give him lots of praise when he performs correctly. Do not rush back inside as soon as he has finished; your puppy might start to delay in the hope of prolonging his time outside with you. Praise him, have a quick game—and then you can both return indoors.

When accidents happen

No matter how vigilant you are, there are bound to be accidents. If your puppy has an accident, always ask yourself: Did I give him enough opportunity? What should I do differently? If you witness the accident, take your puppy outside immediately, and give him praise if he finishes his business out there. If you are not there when he has an accident, do not scold him when you discover what has happened. He will not remember what he has done and will not understand why you are angry. Simply clean it up and resolve to be more vigilant next time.

Choosing a diet

A well-balanced diet is key to your Poodle's health and well-being, so you need to learn a few things about dog food. There are so many different types of food, all claiming to be the best. But which is the best for your Poodle?

Dry food

Most dry foods, or kibble, are scientifically formulated to meet all your dog's nutritional needs. Kibble is certainly convenient, and is often less expensive than other diets.

There are many brands of kibble available, and most offer life-stage foods, such as puppy, adult, and senior. There are also special diets for pregnant bitches, working dogs, and prescription diets for weight control, and other health-related conditions.

Which kibble is best? This is a difficult question, and the best plan is to seek advice from your puppy's breeder or your veterinarian. Generally, an adult maintenance diet should contain 21 to 24 percent protein and 10 to 14 percent fat. Protein levels should be higher in puppy diets, and reduced in senior diets.

Kibble can be fed on its own, or along with other types of food. It is best fed in a puzzle toy—a toy dogs must manipulate in some way to get the food out. No dog is too young—or too old!—to start eating kibble from a puzzle toy.

Canned food and pouches

Canned food contains a lot more water than kibble. Some canned foods—although certainly not all—will have fewer carbohydrates than kibble. The more natural wet foods contain rice rather than other cereals containing gluten, so select this type to avoid allergic reactions. Read the label carefully so you are aware of the ingredients and, remember, what you put in will affect what comes out.

Canned food can be all or part of your dog's diet. Even if it is only a part, the label should say the diet is complete and balanced.

Raw diets

Commercially prepared raw diets may come fresh or frozen or freeze-dried, or you might choose to prepare your dog's diet yourself. They typically contain raw meat, bones, organ meats, fat, vegetables, and sometimes, some cooked grains. Proponents of raw diets believe they are providing the dog with a food that is very close to the natural diet he would eat in the wild.

If you're buying a commercial raw diet, look for a statement on the label that says it's complete and balanced. If you want to prepare the diet yourself, work with a veterinary nutritionist to formulate a healthy diet for your dog. There are a lot of raw diet recipes on the Internet, but recent research has found that the majority of them do not offer complete and balanced nutrition.

Feeding schedule

When your puppy arrives in his new home, he will need four meals evenly spaced throughout the day. You may decide to stick with the food recommended by your puppy's breeder, and if your pup is thriving there is no need to change. However, if your puppy is not doing well on the food, or you have problems with supply, you will need to make a change.

When switching diets, it is very important to do it gradually, changing over from one food to the next a little at a time, and spreading the transition over a week to 10 days. This will avoid the risk of digestive upset.

When your puppy is around 12 weeks, you can cut out one of his meals. He may well have started to leave some of his food, indicating he is ready to do this.

By six months, he can move on to two meals a day—a regime that will suit him for the rest of his life. With Toy Poodles, however, you may find your dog does better on three meals. His little tummy simply can't hold much food at a single meal.

Picky eaters

If your Poodle is reluctant to eat, especially during the settling-in period, it is only natural to try to tempt his appetite. One look from those dark eyes is enough to melt your heart, stirring you to greater efforts to find a food that he will really like. At first you may add some gravy, then you may try some chicken. The clever Poodle will quickly realize that if he holds out, tastier treats will follow.

This is a bad game to play, because you will quickly run out of tempting delicacies. If your dog is turning up his nose at mealtimes, give him 10 minutes to eat what he wants, and then take up his bowl and give him fresh food at his next meal. Do not feed him treats between meals. If you continue this plan for a couple of days, your Poodle will realize that there is nothing to be gained by holding out for better food.

If, however, your dog refuses all food for more than 24 hours, you

need to observe his behavior to see if there are any signs of ill health, which may require a trip to the veterinarian. Puppies, especially, need to eat often and can fade very quickly, so be vigilant.

Bones and chews

Puppies love to chew, and many adult dogs also enjoy gnawing on a bone. A raw marrow bone is ideal, but make sure it is always given under supervision. Rawhide chews are best avoided; it is all too easy for a dog—even a tiny Toy Poodle—to bite off a chunk and swallow it, with the danger of it then causing a blockage.

Ideal weight

To keep your Poodle in good health, you must monitor his weight. Obesity is a major problem among the canine population, and a dog who is fed too much, often coupled with insufficient exercise, is likely to pile on the pounds.

A dog who is carrying too much weight is vulnerable to many health problems. He has a poor quality of life because he cannot exercise properly, and he will almost certainly have a reduced life expectancy.

The Poodle's close-fitting coat makes it fairly easy to assess his condition. When looking at your dog from above, you should be able to see a definite "waist." You should be able to feel his ribs but not see them.

To keep a check on your Poodle's weight, get into the habit of visiting your vet clinic once a month just to weigh your dog. You can keep a record and adjust his diet, if necessary.

If you are concerned that your Poodle is putting on too much weight, or if you think he is underweight, consult your vet, who will help you plan a suitable diet.

Chapter 6

Caring for Your Poodle

The Poodle is a relatively straightforward breed to care for in terms of feeding and exercise—but coat care is another matter. If you do not have time and money to spend on regular trips to the groomer, this is not the breed for you. Even with regular trips to the groomer, though, your Poodle will need some routine care from you.

Coat care

The Poodle's tightly curled, non-shedding coat is a feature of the breed—and one that demands ongoing attention. A pet dog will not need the huge amount of work that is involved in presenting a dog for the show ring, but you need to budget for trips to the groomer every four to six weeks for your Poodle's entire life.

She needs to learn to accept being groomed, bathed, clipped, and trimmed, which means you need to accustom your puppy to being handled from an early age. The breeder will have already started this

process so, hopefully, you will be building on a good foundation.

The first step is to get your puppy used to being handled. Initially, he may wriggle and attempt to mouth you, but just ignore his protests. Hold him steady for a few moments, and reward him when he is still. A puppy needs to learn that it is okay to be touched all over; if you fail to do this, he may try to warn you off by growling, which could develop into more problematic behavior.

Start by handling your puppy all over, stroking him from his head to his tail. Lift up each paw in turn, and reward him with a treat when he cooperates. Then roll him over on to his back and tickle his tummy; this is a very vulnerable position for a dog to adopt, so do not force the issue. Be firm but gentle, and give your Poodle lots of praise when he does as you ask.

When you start grooming, place your puppy on a rubber mat to prevent him from slipping. If you have a Miniature or a Toy Poodle, you may find it easier on your back to place him on a table with a mat. Reward him for standing calmly on the table.

The puppy's coat changes as he matures. To begin with it will be soft and fluffy, then it changes in texture, becoming coarser and

more dense. Initially, all you need to do is work through the coat with a slicker brush (a flat brush with bent wire pins). As the adult coat comes through, you need a metal-toothed comb so you can comb through the hair from the root, which helps to prevent matting and also loosens dead hair. There are a number of trims to choose from but all include leaving some areas of long hair, such as on the ears and tail. To keep these in good order you will need a wire rake brush.

Keeping your Poodle groomed helps keep her clean. No matter what clip she's in or how often she visits the groomer, your Poodle will need to be brushed every day. Start by brushing your Poodle from front to back and head to toe with a slicker brush. Pay close attention to her feet and hindquarters, since this is where mats often form.

Remove any mats with a metal comb. Holding the hair away from the skin and comb it from the end back toward the skin. Be careful not to pull or tug on the hair.

Puppy clip

To begin with, your Poodle will have a puppy clip. The feet, face, and tail are clipped and the body hair is kept long, but is trimmed into shape with scissors. A show dog will stay in a puppy clip until 12 months of age. A pet dog may keep this clip for life.

The puppy cut is a simple cut that basically requires cutting the tips of the hair and keeping the natural shape. Just about any Poodle owner can do this cut themselves, if they are so inclined. Ask your groomer to show you how, or search for how-to videos on YouTube.

Other Poodle clips

The type of trim you choose will largely depend on whether you are keeping your Poodle as a pet or whether she is destined for the show ring. After the puppy clip, these are the most popular clips for pet and show Poodles.

Sporting/utility

This is the most popular clip for pet Poodles, as it looks great and is easy to manage between trips to the groomer. The feet and face are clipped. The body is clipped with a coarser blade to give a close, woolly appearance. The hair on the lower legs is left longer and is scissored into bracelets or socks.

Lamb clip

Another good choice for pet owners. The feet and face are clipped, then the body is clipped with a coarser blade and the legs are trimmed into trousers using scissors.

Puppy lion

A prospective show dog will move from the puppy clip to the puppy lion clip. The coat from the last rib is cut to a shorter length with scissors, while the back legs are shaped following the contours of the joints. The front legs are given a neat trim, blending into the chest hair.

Lion

This is the traditional clip for adult show dogs. The feet, face, and base of the tail are clipped close. The front legs are clipped from the elbow to just above the wrist joint, and there is a mane of hair on the chest that is sculpted into a ball-like shape. The back legs have three bracelets, which are scissored into shape.

Continental

This is another style for show dogs (left). The feet, face, and front legs follow the same lines as the lion clip. But the back legs are shaved close to the lower bracelet (on the hock joint) and a sculpted ring of hair is left on the hip bone.

Bathing

Most breeds do not need regular bathing, as it destroys the natural oils in the coat. This does not apply to the non-shedding Poodle coat. A pet Poodle will need to be bathed every four to six weeks. You may ask the groomer to do the job, for you or you may prefer to do it yourself at home. Obviously, the smaller the Poodle, the easier it is!

Make sure you use a shampoo specially formulated for dogs, and it is also worth investing in a good-quality conditioner. Your Poodle's coat needs to be thoroughly groomed so that it is free from mats before you bathe him. Water must be at your body temperature, and you need to make sure you rinse out all traces of shampoo and conditioner. Blot as much moisture as you can with a towel and then dry the coat with a hair dryer.

Routine care

In addition to grooming, you will need to carry out some other routine care.

Eyes

Check the eyes for signs of soreness or discharge. If there is debris around the eye, you can use a piece of cotton—a separate piece for each eye—to wipe it away. If there is discharge from the eye, you should schedule a visit to the vet, who can examine the eyes and prescribe the appropriate treatment.

Ears

Checking ears is essential with a Poodle, because hair tends to grow inside the ear. This needs to be plucked out; otherwise it can become dirty and act as a source of infection. Apply a little ear powder (available from pet supply stores) inside the ear, and this will make it easier for you to grip the hair with finger and thumb and pluck it out.

If the ear is dirty, you can clean it using a damp cotton pad. Be careful not to probe into the ear canal or you could do more harm than good. If your dog's ears appear to be particularly dirty and foul-smelling, consult your vet, who will prescribe the appropriate treatment.

Teeth

Dental disease is increasing among dogs, which is why teeth cleaning should be an essential part of your care regime. This is particularly the case with Toy dogs, who are prone to dental problems. The build-up of tartar on the teeth can result in tooth decay, gum infection, and bad breath, and if it is allowed to accumulate, your dog will need to have her teeth cleaned under anesthesia.

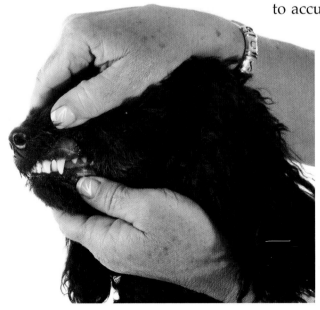

When your Poodle is still a puppy, accustom her to teeth cleaning so it becomes routine. Dog toothpaste comes in a variety of meaty flavors that your Poodle will like, so you can start by putting toothpaste on your finger and gently rubbing her teeth. You can then progress to using a finger brush or a toothbrush, whichever you find most convenient.

Remember to reward your Poodle when she cooperates, and she will positively look forward to her teeth-cleaning sessions.

Nails

Nail trimming is a task dreaded by many owners—and many dogs— but again, if you start early and are gentle, your Poodle will get used to the task and will not fight against it.

Poodles generally have dark or black nails, which means you cannot see the quick—the bundle of nerves and blood vessels that runs through the nail. This makes nail trimming more difficult, because you need to

avoid cutting into the quick. If you do this accidentally, it is not disastrous, but it will cause the nail to bleed profusely. This will also hurt your Poodle, and she will remember it next time you attempt to trim her nails. The best policy is to trim little and often, so the nails don't grow too long and you do not risk cutting too much and nicking the quick.

If you are worried about trimming your Poodle's nails, go to your vet so you can see it done properly. If you are still concerned, you can always ask the groomer to do it.

Exercise

The exercise your Poodle requires will depend on her size, and this may well have influenced the variety you choose. Obviously, the Standard need the most exercise. This is a dog who loves to run. She is an excellent swimmer and is very inquisitive. She will relish the opportunity to investigate her surroundings.

However, exercise needs to be limited during the vulnerable growing phase, as too much stress on the joints can result in permanent damage. To begin with, a puppy will get as much exercise as she needs playing in your yard and going on short leash walks. This can be increased gradually to short bursts of free running and some longer leash walking. When fully mature, the Standard Poodle will enjoy as much exercise as you can give her.

The Miniature is more robust than the Toy, and is very adaptable in her exercise requirements. She will enjoy the chance to run and explore, but will also be content with less, as long as she is given plenty of mental stimulation. Leash walks every day and occasional off-leash runs will do.

The Toy Poodle is very low maintenance when it comes to exercise, but her needs should not be neglected. Leash walks every day are still a must. She may not want to walk for miles, but she will certainly appreciate the stimulation of being taken out and about.

Playing games

This is a great way of providing physical exercise and mental stimulation. The Poodle is playful and inquisitive, and she will love interacting with you and earning rewards. The more you play with her, the more she will enjoy it. The two of you can become increasingly inventive with games of search and retrieve, and maybe some trick training thrown in for good measure.

If your Poodle is a bit of a

foodie, there is a game you can play that will use her mental energies and make use of her sense of smell. Once in a while, do not give your Poodle her food in a bowl; instead, scatter it over a small area in the house or yard. Let your Poodle see what you are doing, and then encourage her to find her dinner. There are few dogs who can resist this, and they will positively relish the task of seeking out their food.

The older Poodle

We are fortunate that Poodles enjoy a good life expectancy. However, it is inevitable that your Poodle will slow up as she gets older. You'll need to keep a close eye on her to monitor when this change occurs. The older Poodle may sleep more and she may be reluctant to go for longer walks. She may show signs of stiffness when she gets up from her bed, but these generally ease when she starts moving.

Some older Poodles may have impaired vision, and some may become a little deaf, but as long as their senses do not deteriorate dramatically, this is something older dogs learn to live with.

If you treat your older dog with kindness and consideration, she will enjoy her later years and suffer the minimum of discomfort. It is advisable to switch her over to a senior diet, which is more suited to her needs, and you may have to adjust the quantity, as she will not be burning as many calories as she did when he was younger and more energetic. Make sure her sleeping quarters are warm and free

from drafts, and if she gets wet, make sure you dry her thoroughly.

Most important of all, be guided by your Poodle. She will have good days when she feels up to going for a walk, and other days when she would prefer to poke around in the yard.

If you have a younger dog at home, this may stimulate your Poodle to take more of an interest in what is going on. But make sure she is not pestered, as she needs to rest undisturbed when she is tired.

Letting go

Inevitably there comes a time when your Poodle is not enjoying a good quality of life, and you need to make the painful decision to let her go. We all wish that our dogs died painlessly in their sleep, but unfortunately, this is rarely the case. However, we can allow our dogs to die with dignity, and to suffer as a little as possible. This should be our way of saying thank you for the wonderful companionship they have given us.

When you feel the time is drawing close, talk to your veterinarian, who will be able to make an objective assessment of your Poodle's condition and will help you to make the right decision.

This is the hardest thing you will ever have to do as a dog owner, and it is only natural to grieve for your beloved Poodle. But eventually, you will be able to look back on the happy memories of times spent together, and this will bring much comfort.

You may, in time, feel that your life is not complete without a Poodle, and you will feel ready to welcome a new dog into your home.

Chapter 7

Training
Your Poodle

To live in the modern world without fear and anxieties, a Poodle needs to receive an education in social skills, so that he learns to cope calmly and confidently in a wide variety of situations.

The Standard can appear intimidating because of his size, so it is essential that he learn self-control. The Toy and Miniature are small enough to go just about everywhere with their owners, so they need to learn how to be model canine citizens as well.

Early learning

The breeder will have begun a program of socialization by getting the puppies used to all the sights and sounds of a busy household. You need to continue this when your pup arrives in his new home, making sure he is not worried by household appliances, such as the vacuum cleaner and the washing machine, and that he gets

used to unexpected noises from the stereo and television.

To begin with, your puppy needs to get used to all the members of his new family, but then you should give him the opportunity to meet friends and other people who come to the house.

If you do not have children of your own, make sure your puppy has the chance to meet and play with other people's children—making sure interactions are always supervised—so he learns that humans come in small sizes too.

Home alone

The Poodle adores his family, and within weeks of arriving in his new home, he will form a strong bond with his humans. This is just what you want. But be careful. A Poodle also needs to learn to cope on his own, otherwise he will develop separation anxiety. This happens when a dog panics when he is left on his own because he fears he is being abandoned.

Instead of settling quietly until his family returns, the anxious dog will become increasingly distressed. He may bark or whine constantly, he may become destructive, and he may even soil his sleeping quarters.

This should never be seen as a sign of how much your Poodle loves you. It is, in fact, a sign of acute distress. Right from the start, you need to get your dog used to spending short periods on his own.

Ideally, settle him in his crate with a boredom-busting toy, such as a Kong filled with food, and leave him alone for a short period. When you return, do not make a big fuss over him. You might even wait a few minutes before you go to his crate, just to let him know that you are back but it's no big deal.

Gradually increase the amount of time you leave your Poodle, so that you are confident he will settle happily for a couple of hours.

Keep leaving rituals to a minimum, so your Poodle does not start getting worried as he anticipates your departure, and will be relaxed and calm when you return. This way your Poodle will learn that arrivals and departures are part of daily life and are not a cause for anxiety.

The outside world

When your puppy has completed his vaccinations, he is ready to venture into the wider world. As a breed, the Poodle is generally confident and self-assured, but there is a lot for a youngster to take in, so do not swamp him with too many new experiences when you first set out.

And of course, you need to work on leash training before you go on your first expedition. There will be plenty of distractions to deal with, so you do not want additional problems of coping with a dog who is pulling or lagging on the leash. Spend some time training, and you can set off with your Poodle walking by your side on a loose leash.

He may need additional encouragement when you venture farther afield, so arm yourself with some extra special treats, which will

give him a good reason to focus on you when you need him to.

Start walking your puppy in a quiet area with light traffic, and only progress to a busier place when he is ready. There is so much to see and hear—people (maybe carrying bags or umbrellas), strollers, bicycles, cars, trucks, machinery—so give your puppy a chance to take it all in.

If he does appear worried, do not fall into the trap of sympathizing with him, or worse still, picking him up. This is almost a reflex reaction if you have a Toy Poodle, but it is not helpful. Regardless of size, a dog must learn to stand on his own four feet and not become dependent on back-up from his owner.

Instead of picking up your Poodle to "rescue" him, give him a little space so he does not have to confront whatever he is frightened of, and distract him with a few treats. Then ask him to walk past, using an encouraging tone of voice, never forcing him by yanking on the leash. Reward him for any forward movement, and your puppy will soon learn that he can trust you and there is nothing to fear.

Dog to dog meetings

Your pup also needs to continue his education in canine manners, which was started by his mother and by his littermates, as he must be able to greet all dogs calmly, giving the signals that say he is friendly.

The extrovert Standard Poodle tends to think that everyone is his friend. This can be slightly alarming when he is interacting with smaller dogs, so he needs to signal clearly that his intentions are friendly. The Toy and Miniature Poodle are naturally sociable but, in the case of the Toy, owners can worry about interactions with bigger dogs and often intervene—needlessly exacerbating the situation. It is important to treat a Toy Poodle just as you would any other dog and make sure he develops good canine meeting and greeting skills.

With all sizes, find a friend who has a dog with a solid temperament and visit their house. Allow the two dogs to play outside for 10 minutes or so. Do not prolong the game, as you do not want your youngster to become over-excited or overwhelmed.

Once the two dogs have had a few play dates at home, go for a walk and allow them to exercise together off leash. They will interact with each other, but their focus will shift periodically as they will be distracted by other sights and smells.

Extend your Poodle's circle of acquaintances by finding other friends who have dogs of sound temperament, ideally representing a number of different breeds, sizes, and types. The more your Poodle practices meeting and greeting, the better he will become at reading body language and assessing other dogs' intentions.

Training classes

A training class will give your Poodle the opportunity to work alongside other dogs in a controlled situation, and he will also learn to focus on you in a different, distracting environment. Both these lessons will be vital as your dog matures.

However, the training class needs to be well run, or you risk doing more harm than good. Before you go along with your puppy, attend a class as an observer to make sure you are happy with what goes on. Find out:

- How much training experience do the instructors have?
- Are the classes divided into appropriate age and size categories?
- Do they use positive, reward-based training methods?
- Do any of the instructors have experience with Poodles?

If the training class is well run, it is certainly worth attending. Both you and your Poodle will learn useful training exercises. It will increase his social skills, and you will have the chance to talk to lots of like-minded dog lovers.

Training guidelines

The Poodle is a clever dog and is quick to learn. This is true of all three varieties, so do not make the mistake of thinking that a tiny Toy Poodle does not need training. He may be easier to manage than a young, exuberant Standard Poodle, but he requires mental stimulation and basic training in good manners in exactly the same way.

Regardless of which variety you have, make training a priority and, above all, make it fun!

You will be keen to get started, but in your rush to get training underway, do not forget the fundamentals that could make the difference between success and failure. You need to get into the mindset of a Poodle, figuring out what motivates him and, equally, what makes him switch off. Decide on your priorities for training, set realistic goals, and then think of ways to make your training positive and rewarding.

When you start training, try to observe the following guidelines:

- Choose an area that is free from distractions so your puppy will focus on you. You can progress to a more challenging environment as your pup progresses.
- Do not train your puppy just after he has eaten or exercised. He will either be too full, or too tired, to concentrate.
- Do not train if you are in a bad mood, or if you are short of time—these sessions always end in disaster!
- Providing a worthwhile reward is an essential tool in training. You will probably get the best results if you use some extra special food treats, although some Poodles get very focused on toys, and will see a game with a favorite toy as a top reward.
- If you decide to use a toy, make sure it is only brought out for training sessions, so it accrues added value.

- Keep your verbal cues simple, and always use the same one for each exercise. For example, when you ask your puppy to go into the Down position, the cue is "Down," not "Lie Down," "Get Down," or anything else. Remember, your Poodle does not speak English; he associates the sound of the word with the action.

- If your dog is finding an exercise difficult, break it down into smaller steps so it is easier to understand.

- Do not make your training sessions boring and repetitious. The Poodle is quick-witted and prefers to work at a fast pace. If training is dull, he will lose focus and go off to find something more interesting to do.

- Do not train for too long, particularly with a young puppy, who has a very short attention span.

- Always end training sessions on a positive note. This does not necessarily mean getting an exercise right. If your pup is tired and making mistakes, ask him to do a simple exercise so you have the opportunity to praise and reward him. You may find that he benefits from having a break and will make better progress next time you try.

Remember that if your Poodle is rewarded for a behavior, he is

likely to repeat it—so make sure you are 100 percent consistent and always reward the behavior you want to see.

First lessons

Like all puppies, a young Poodle will soak up new experiences like a sponge, so training should start from the time your pup arrives in his new home.

Wearing a collar

You may or may not want your Poodle to wear a collar all the time—this may depend on whether you are keeping him in a show clip or a pet clip. But when he goes out in public he will need to be on a leash, and so he should be used to the feel of a collar around his neck. Get your pup used to wearing a soft nylon collar for a few minutes at a time, until it's no big deal.

Fit the collar so that you can get at least two fingers between the collar and his neck. Then have a game to distract his attention. This will work for a few moments. Then he will stop and start scratching away at the peculiar thing around his neck. Bend down, rotate the collar, pat him on the head, and distract him by playing with a toy or giving him a treat.

After he has worn the collar for a few minutes each day, he will soon ignore it. Remember, never leave the collar on the puppy unsupervised, especially when he is outside in the yard, or when he is in his crate, as it is could get snagged, causing serious injury.

Walking on the leash

This is a simple exercise that all dogs need to master. You may find that a Standard is more likely to pull ahead, whereas a Toy or a Miniature may need a little more encouragement. In all situations, the best plan is to learn the basics at home before venturing into the outside world where there is so much to distract him.

Once your puppy is used to the collar, take him outside into a secure area, such as your backyard, where there are no distractions. Attach the leash and, to begin with, allow him to wander with the leash trailing, making sure it does not become snagged. Then pick up the leash and follow the pup where he wants to go; he needs to get used to the sensation of being attached to you.

The next stage is to get your Poodle to follow you, and for this you will need some treats. To give yourself the best chance of success, make sure the treats are high value, so your Poodle is motivated to work with you.

Show him you have a treat in your hand, and then encourage him to follow you. Walk a few paces, and if he is walking with you, stop and reward him. If he puts on the brakes, simply change direction and lure him with the treat.

Next, introduce some changes of direction so your puppy is walking confidently alongside you. At this stage, introduce the verbal cue "Heel" when your puppy is in the correct position.

You can then graduate to walking your puppy away from home, starting in quiet areas and building up to busier environments. If you are struggling with your Toy Poodle on the leash, resist taking the easy option of picking him up. This solves the immediate problem, but you are heading for trouble, as your Poodle will learn that jamming on the brakes means he instantly gets picked up. Instead, arm yourself with lots of tasty treats, and give yourself plenty of time so you can reward your pup for cooperating. He is then more likely to repeat the behavior you want from him in the future.

Come when called

The Poodle loves people—but he is a clever, curious dog and is keen to explore his surroundings. There are so many enticing smells out there, other dogs to meet and greet, plus people who might pet or play with him—so you can understand why he may not always want to come to you when you call.

The key to successful recall training is to start early, and to teach your Poodle to focus on you, regardless of distractions.

Hopefully, the breeder will have laid the foundations simply by calling the puppies to "Come" when it is dinnertime, or when they are moving from one place to another. You can build on this when your puppy arrives in your home, calling him to "Come" when he is in a confined space, such as the kitchen. This is a good place to build up a positive association with the verbal cue—particularly if you ask your puppy to "Come" to get his dinner!

The next stage is to transfer the lesson to a secure outdoor space, such as your backyard. Arm yourself with some treats, and wait until your puppy is distracted. Then call him, using a higher-pitched, excited tone of voice. At this stage, a puppy wants to be with you, so capitalize on this and keep practicing the verbal cue, and rewarding your puppy with a treat and lots of praise when he comes, so he knows it is worth his while to come to you.

Now you are ready to introduce some distractions. Try calling him when someone else is in the yard, or wait a few minutes until he is investigating a really interesting scent. If your puppy responds, immediately reward him with a treat. If he is slow to come, run away a few steps and then call again, making yourself sound really exciting. Jump up and down, open your arms wide to welcome him; it doesn't matter how silly you look, he needs to see you as the most fun person in the world.

When you have a reliable recall in the yard, you can venture into the outside world. Do not be too ambitious to begin with; try a recall in a quiet place with the minimum of distractions so you can be assured of success.

Do not make the mistake of asking your dog to come only at the end of his off-leash exercise or time in the yard. What is the incentive in coming back to you if all you do is clip on his leash, marking the end of his free time? Instead, call your dog at random times, giving him a treat and a pat, and then letting him go free again. This way, he learns coming to you—and focusing on you—is always rewarding.

Stationary exercises

The Sit and Down are easy to teach, and mastering these exercises will be rewarding for both you and your Poodle. They are useful in a wide variety of situations and mean you will always have a measure of control over your dog—for his own safety and everyone else's.

Sit

The best way to teach this cue is to lure your Poodle into position, and for this you can use a treat or his food bowl as the reward. Hold the reward above his head and move it slightly back. As he looks up, he will lower his hindquarters and go into a sit.

Practice this a few times, and when your puppy understands what the exercise is about, introduce the verbal cue, "Sit."

When your Poodle understands the exercise, he will respond to the verbal cue alone, and you will not need to lure or even reward him every time he sits. However, it is a good idea to give him treats at random times when he cooperates, to keep him guessing! And *always* reward him with praise, so he knows he's made the right choice.

Down

This is an important lesson, and can be a lifesaver if an emergency arises and you need to bring your Poodle to an instant halt.

This is an easier exercise to teach if you start with your dog in a Sit. Stand or kneel in front of him and show him you have a treat in your hand. Hold the treat just in front of his nose and slowly lower it toward the ground, between his front legs. As your Poodle follows the treat, he will go down on his front legs and, in a few moments, his hindquarters will follow.

Close your hand over the treat so he doesn't cheat and get the treat before he is in the correct position. As soon as he is all the way Down, give him the treat and lots of praise. Keep practicing, and when your Poodle understands what you want, introduce the verbal cue "Down."

Control exercises

Dogs do not always find self-control easy, and these exercises are not the most exciting. But they will make your dog much easier to live with. And he will understand that he will be rewarded for cooperating with you.

Wait

This exercise teaches your Poodle to wait in position until you give him another cue. It differs from the Stay exercise, where he must stay where you have left him for a longer period.

The most useful application of "Wait" is when you are walking him and need him to wait at the curb, or are getting your dog out of the car and you need him to stay in position until you clip on his leash.

Start with your puppy on the leash to give you a greater chance of success. Ask him to "Sit," then stand at his side. Take one step forward and hold your hand back behind you, palm facing the dog. Step back, release him with a word, such as "Okay," and then reward him.

Clicker Training

There are many different methods of training, and as long as the methods you use are positive and reward-based, you will not go wrong.

You may decide you want to try clicker training—a modern approach that has proved very effective. The clicker is the size of a matchbox, fitted with a small device that makes a clicking noise when it is pressed. The dog is taught that a click means a reward will follow, so he quickly learns to work for a click. The benefit is that the click enables us to precisely mark exactly the behavior we are trying to elicit. Then, even if we're slow with the treat, the message has been delivered.

As a trainer, you need to get your timing right and click at the precise moment your dog does what you want, then reward him. This way, your dog will repeat the desired behavior, knowing that he will earn a click and then get a treat. Clicker training is easy with puppies, and adult dogs too.

Practice this a few times, waiting a little longer before you reward him, and then introduce the verbal cue "Wait." You can reinforce the lesson by using it in different situations, such as asking your Poodle to "Wait" before you put his food bowl down.

Stay

You need to differentiate this exercise from the Wait by using a different hand signal and a different verbal cue.

Start with your Poodle in the Down, as he most likely to be secure in this position. Face him and take one step back, holding your hand, palm flat, facing him. Wait a second and then come back to stand in front of him.

Practice until your Poodle understands the exercise, and then introduce the verbal cue "Stay." Gradually increase the distance between you and your puppy, and increase the challenge by walking around him—and even stepping over him—so that he learns he must "Stay" until you release him, using your release word, "Okay."

Leave

A response to this verbal cue means your Poodle will learn to give up a toy on request, and it follows that he will give up anything when he is asked, which is very useful if he has got hold of a forbidden object such as a shoe or somebody's glove.

This is particularly important with a Poodle, who can become possessive with favorite toys or places of high value, such as the sofa, or even your bed!

The "Leave" command can be taught quite easily when you are first playing with your puppy. As you gently take a toy from his mouth, introduce the verbal cue, "Leave," and then praise him. If he is reluctant, swap the toy for another toy or a treat. This will usually do the trick.

Do not try to pull the toy from his mouth if he refuses to give it up, as you will make the situation confrontational. Let the toy go "dead" in your hand, and then swap it for a new toy, or a really high-value treat, so this becomes the better option.

Remember to make a big fuss over your Poodle when he does as you ask, so he learns that cooperation is always best—and most rewarding—option.

Again the strategy is not to be confrontational but to offer him a better reward, such as a treat or a toy, and then call him to you. As far as the Poodle is concerned, he has not been forced to give up the thing he values; he has simply been offered something better—a win-win situation!

Chapter 8

Keeping Your Poodle Busy

The Poodle is highly intelligent, quick to learn, and loves to show off—so the sky's the limit when it comes to getting involved in canine sports. A few of the most popular canine sports are listed here, but there are many more. There are choices for every size Poodle. The AKC, and well as the Poodle Club of America (listed in Find Out More), are good places to learn about sports for Poodles.

Canine Good Citizen

The American Kennel Club runs the Canine Good Citizen program. It promotes responsible ownership and helps you to train a well-behaved dog who will fit in with the community. The program tests your dog on basic good manners, alone and with other people and dogs around. It's excellent for all pet owners and is also an ideal starting point if you plan to compete with your Poodle in any sport.

Competitive obedience

If your dog is keen to learn the cues you started teaching her as a puppy, she might enjoy competitive obedience. The levels start off being relatively easy and become progressively more challenging, with additional exercises and increasingly minimal instructions from the handler.

Obedience exercises include: heel work at varying paces with dog and handler following a pattern decided by the judge, stays, recalls, retrieves, send-aways, scent discrimination, and distance control.

The intelligent Poodle is more than capable of performing these exercises with distinction. But at the top level a very high degree of precision and accuracy is called for, and this may not always suit the flamboyant nature of the Poodle. Skilled handlers make training fun.

Agility

Agility is basically a canine obstacle course. It is fast and furious and is great for the fitness of both handler and dog. The obstacles include hurdles, long jump, tire jump, tunnels (rigid and collapsible), weaving poles, an A-frame, a dog-walk, and a seesaw.

Agility is judged on the time taken to get around the course, with faults given for knocking down fences, missing obstacles, and going through the course in the wrong order.

Standard Poodles will compete in classes for large dogs; Miniatures and Toys will, generally be categorized as small dogs. The Standard competes with grace and athleticism but when it comes to speed, the Miniature can really motor!

Rally O

This is loosely based on obedience, and also has a few exercises borrowed from agility when you get to the highest levels. Handler and dog must complete a course, in the designated order, that has anywhere from 12 to 20 exercises. The course is timed and the team must finish within the limit, but there are no bonus points for speed. The great advantage of Rally O is that it is very relaxed, and anyone can compete.

Musical freestyle

This is a relatively new discipline that is growing in popularity. Dog and handler must perform a choreographed routine to music, allowing the dog to perform an array of tricks and moves that delight the crowd.

There are two categories: freestyle heeling, where the dog stays close to her handler in a variety of positions; and canine freestyle, where the dog works at a greater distance and performs some of the more spectacular moves.

A panel of judges marks the routine for choreography, accuracy, and musical interpretation. Both categories demand a huge amount of training, but if you keep training sessions light-hearted, with plenty of positive reinforcement, the Poodle will prove to be a real crowd pleaser, and the smaller varieties are at no disadvantage at all!

Flyball

Flyball is a relay race with four dogs on a team. Each dog runs down a 51-foot (15.5 m) course, jumping over four hurdles on the way to a spring-loaded box. The dog trips the lever on the box, a tennis ball pops up, the dog must catch it, and then run back over the four hurdles to the starting line. Then the next dog goes. The fastest team to have all four dogs run without errors, wins.

Small dogs are especially popular on flyball teams, because the hurdles are set at four inches below the shoulder height of the shortest dog—with eight inches (20 cm) as a minimum. Having a Toy Poodle on the team means all the dogs get those eight-inch hurdles.

Showing

The Poodle can be seen in his full glory in the show ring, but this is not an easy breed to show. First, you need a top-quality Poodle who conforms to the breed standard.

Second, you need to be skilled in grooming, clipping, and show presentation, which is an art in itself. Third, you need a Poodle who is a natural show-off and enjoys being in the ring.

A show Poodle needs to be trained to stand in a show pose, to accept a detailed hands-on examination by the judge, and to move correctly on a show leash, following a pattern indicated by the judge. Ringcraft classes will teach you how to do this, and will also give you a good grounding in show etiquette.

Tracking

In organized tracking events, dogs must learn to follow scent trails of varying ages, over different types of terrain. These become increasingly tougher as a dog works her way through the levels. Poodles, even the small varieties, generally have a wonderful sense of smell. They enjoy working scent, and learn "nose games" quickly.

Working and Hunting Tests

The Poodle Club of America offers working tests that evaluate the Poodle's interest in birds, ability to take direction from his handler, willingness to enter the water, and general trainability.

Standard Poodles can also participate in AKC spaniel and retriever hunting tests, and in upland hunting tests for working retrievers.

Chapter 9

Poodle Health Care

Regardless of size, the Poodle is an active dog and, with a good diet, a comprehensive program of preventive care and good management, he should suffer few significant health problems.

Parasites

No matter how well you look after your Poodle, you will have to accept that parasites—internal and external—are ever present, and you need to take preventive action.

Internal parasites live inside your dog. These are the various worms. Most will find a home in the digestive tract, but there is also a parasite that lives in the heart. If infestation is unchecked, a dog's health will be severely jeopardized, but routine preventive treatment is simple and effective.

External parasites live on your dog's body—in his skin and fur, and sometimes in his ears.

Roundworm

This is found in the small intestine. Signs of infestation will be

Vaccination Program

The American Animal Hospital Association and the American Veterinary Medical Association have issued vaccination guidelines that apply to all breeds of dogs. They divide the available vaccines into two groups: core vaccines, which every dog should get, and non-core vaccines, which are optional.

Core vaccines are canine parvovirus-2, distemper, and adenovirus-2. Puppies should get vaccinated every three to four weeks between the ages of 6 and 16 weeks, with the final dose at 14 to 16 weeks of age. If a dog older than 16 weeks is getting their first vaccine, one dose is enough. Dogs who received an initial dose at less than 16 weeks should be given a booster after one year, and then every three years or more thereafter.

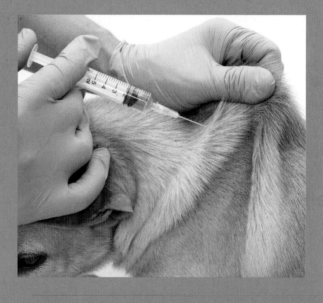

Rabies is also a core vaccine. For puppies less than 16 weeks old, a single dose should be given no earlier than 12 weeks of age. Revaccination is recommended annually or every three years, depending on the vaccine used and state and local laws.

Non-core vaccines are canine parainfluenza virus, Bordetella bronchiseptica, canine influenza virus, canine measles, leptospirosis, and Lyme disease.

The dog's exposure risk, lifestyle, and geographic location all come into play when deciding which non-core vaccines may be appropriate for your dog. Have a conversation with your veterinarian about the right vaccine protocol for your dog.

a poor coat, a potbelly, diarrhea, and lethargy. Prospective mothers should be treated before mating, but it is almost inevitable that parasites she may have will be passed on to the puppies. For this reason, a breeder will start a worming program, which you will need to continue. Ask your vet for advice on treatment, which will need to continue throughout your dog's life.

Tapeworm

Infection occurs when the dog ingests fleas or lice. The adult worm takes up residence in the small intestine, releasing mobile segments (which contain eggs), which can be seen in a dog's feces as small rice-like grains. The only other obvious sign of infestation is irritation of the anus. Again, routine preventive treatment is required throughout your dog's life.

Heartworm

This parasite is transmitted by mosquitoes, and is found in all parts of the USA, although its prevalence does vary. Heartworms live in the right side of the heart and larvae can grow up to 14 inches (35 cm) long. A dog with heartworm is at severe risk from heart failure, so preventive treatment, as advised by your vet, is essential. Dogs should also have regular tests to check for the presence of infection.

Lungworm

Lungworm is a parasite that lives in the heart and major

blood vessels supplying the lungs. It can cause many problems, such as breathing difficulties, excessive bleeding, sickness, diarrhea, seizures, and even death. The dog becomes infected when ingesting slugs and snails, often accidentally when rummaging through undergrowth. Lungworm is not common, but it is on the increase and a responsible owner should be aware of it. Fortunately, it is easily preventable, and even affected dogs usually make a full recovery if treated early enough. Your vet will be able to advise you on the risks in your area and what form of treatment may be required.

How to Detect Fleas

You may suspect your dog has fleas, but how can you be sure? There are two methods to try. Run a fine comb through your dog's coat, and see if you can detect the presence of fleas on the skin, or clinging to the comb. Alternatively, sit your dog on some white paper and rub his back. This will dislodge feces from the fleas, which will be visible as small brown specks. To double check, shake the specks on to some damp cotton balls. Flea feces consist of the dried blood taken from the host, so if the specks turn a lighter shade of red, you know your dog has fleas.

Fleas

A dog may carry many types of fleas. The flea stays on the dog only long enough to feed and breed, but its presence will result in itching. If your dog has an allergy to fleas—usually a reaction to the flea's saliva—he will scratch himself until he is raw. Spot-ons and chewable flea preventives are easy to use and highly effective, and should be given regularly to prevent fleas entirely. Some also prevent ticks.

If your dog has fleas, talk to your veterinarian about the best treatment. Bear in mind that your entire home, dog's whole environment, and all other pets in your home will also need to be treated.

Ticks

These are blood-sucking parasites that are most frequently found in areas where sheep or deer are present. The main danger is their ability to pass a wide variety of very serious diseases—including Lyme disease—to both dogs and humans. The preventive you give your dog for fleas generally works for ticks, but you should discuss the best product to use with your vet.

Ear mites

These parasites live in the outer ear canal. The signs of infestation are a brown, waxy discharge, and your dog will

often shake his head and scratch his ear. If you suspect your dog has ear mites, a visit to the vet will be needed so that medicated ear drops can be prescribed.

Cheyletiella mange

These small, white mites are visible to the naked eye and are often referred to as "walking dandruff." They cause a scruffy coat and mild itchiness. They are zoonotic—transferable to humans—so prompt treatment with an insecticide prescribed by your veterinarian is essential.

Chiggers

These are picked up from the undergrowth, and can be seen as bright red, yellow, or orange specks on the webbing between the toes, although this can also be found elsewhere on the body, such as on the ear flaps. Treatment is effective with the appropriate insecticide, prescribed by your vet.

Skin mites

There are two types of parasite that burrow into a dog's skin. Demodex canis is transferred from a mother to her pups while they are feeding. Treatment is with a topical preparation, and sometimes antibiotics are needed. Refer to your vet.

The other skin mite is sarcoptes scabiei, which causes intense itching and hair loss. It is highly contagious, so all dogs in a household will need to be treated, which involves repeated bathing with a medicated shampoo.

Common ailments

As with all living animals, dogs can be affected by a variety of ailments. Most can be treated effectively after consulting with your vet, who will prescribe appropriate medication and will advise you on how to care for your dog's needs.

Here are some of the more common problems that could affect your Poodle, with advice on how to deal with them.

Anal glands

These are two small sacs on either side of the anus, which produce a dark brown secretion. The anal glands should empty every time a dog defecates, but if they become blocked or impacted, a dog will experience increasing discomfort. He may lick at his rear end, or scoot his bottom along the ground to relieve the irritation.

Treatment involves a trip to the vet, who will empty the glands manually. It is important to do this without delay or they could become infected.

Dental problems

All three varieties need good dental care, but it is especially important with the Toy Poodle, who is more likely to have problems with teeth and gums.

Regular brushing prevents the accumulation of tartar, which causes gum infection and tooth decay. If tartar accumulates to the extent that you cannot remove it by brushing, your dog will need to be anesthetized for a dental cleaning by the veterinarian.

How to Remove a Tick

If you spot a tick on your dog, do not try to pluck it off, as you risk leaving the hard mouth parts embedded in his skin. The best way to remove a tick is to use a pair of fine tweezers, or you can buy a tick remover. Grasp the tick head firmly and then pull the tick straight out from the skin. If you are using a tick remover, check the instructions, as some recommend a circular twist when pulling. When you have removed the tick, clean the area with mild soap and water.

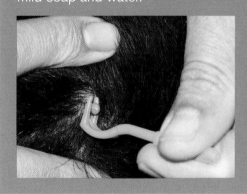

Diarrhea

There are many reasons why a dog might have diarrhea, but most commonly it is the result of scavenging, a sudden change of diet, or an adverse reaction to a particular type of food.

If your dog is suffering from diarrhea, the first step is to withhold food for a day. It is important that he does not become dehydrated,

so make sure fresh drinking water is available. However, drinking too much can increase the diarrhea, which may be accompanied with vomiting, so limit how much he drinks at any one time.

After allowing the stomach to rest, feed a bland diet, such as white fish or chicken with boiled rice for a few days. In most cases, your dog's motions will return to normal and you can resume normal feeding, although this should be done gradually.

However, if this fails to work and the diarrhea persists for more than a few days, you should consult your vet. Your dog may have an infection, which needs to be treated with antibiotics, or the diarrhea may indicate some other problem that needs expert diagnosis.

Ear infections

The Poodle's ears lie close to his head, so air cannot circulate as freely as it would in a dog with ears that stand up. Therefore, it is important to clean them regularly, because dirty ears can become infected.

A healthy ear is clean, with no sign of redness or inflammation, and no evidence of a waxy brown discharge or a foul odor. If you see your dog scratching her ear, shaking her head, or holding one ear at an odd angle, you will need to consult your vet. The most likely causes are ear mites, an infection, or there may a foreign body, such as a grass seed, trapped in the ear.

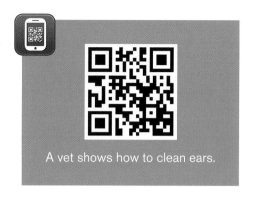

A vet shows how to clean ears.

Depending on the cause, treatment is with medicated ear drops, possibly containing antibiotics. If a foreign body is suspected, the vet will need to carry out further investigation.

Eye problems

Healthy eyes are bright and sparkling with no sign of discharge. If your Poodle's eyes look red and sore, he is likely to be suffering from conjunctivitis. This may, or may not be accompanied with a watery or a crusty discharge. Conjunctivitis can be caused by a bacterial or viral infection, it could be the result of an injury, or it could be an adverse reaction to pollen.

You will need to consult your vet for a correct diagnosis, but in the case of an infection, treatment with medicated eye drops is effective.

Conjunctivitis may also be the first sign of more serious inherited eye problems, which will be discussed later in this chapter.

In some instances, a dog may suffer from a dry, itchy eye, which he may further injure by scratching. This condition, known as keratoconjunctivitis sicca, may be inherited.

Foreign bodies

In the home, puppies—and some older dogs—cannot resist chewing anything that looks interesting. The toys you choose for your dog should be suitably robust to withstand damage, but children's toys can be irresistible.

Some dogs will chew—and swallow—anything from socks and other items from the laundry basket to golf balls and stones from the garden. Obviously, these items are indigestible and could cause an obstruction in your dog's intestine, which is potentially lethal.

The signs to look for are vomiting and a tucked-up posture. The dog will often be restless and will look as if he is in pain. In this situation, you must get your dog to the vet without delay, as surgery will be needed to remove the obstruction.

Heatstroke

When the temperature rises, make sure your dog always has access to shady areas, and wait for a cooler part of the day before going for a walk. Never leave your dog in the car, as the temperature can rise dramatically—even on a cloudy day. Heatstroke can

happen very rapidly, and unless you are able to lower your dog's temperature, it can be fatal.

The signs of heatstroke include heavy panting and difficulty breathing, bright red tongue and mucous membranes, thick saliva, and vomiting. Eventually, the dog becomes progressively unsteady and passes out.

If your dog appears to be suffering from heatstroke, this is a true emergency. Lie him flat and then cool him as quickly as possible by hosing him down or covering him with wet towels. As soon as he has made some recovery, take him to the vet.

Lameness or limping

There are a wide variety of reasons why a dog might go lame, from a simple muscle strain to a fracture, ligament damage, or more complex problems with the joints, including inherited disorders. It takes an expert to make a correct diagnosis, so if you are concerned about your dog, do not delay in seeking help.

As your dog becomes elderly, he may suffer from arthritis, which you will see as general stiffness, particularly when he gets up after resting. It will help if you ensure his bed is in a warm, draft-free location, and if your Poodle gets wet after exercise, be sure to dry him thoroughly.

If your elderly dog seems to be in pain, consult your vet, who will be able to help with pain relief medication and nutritional supplements.

Skin problems

The Poodle can be prone to skin problems, which may take the form of hair loss, soreness, and itching. Fleas, and other external parasites can result in itching, and the skin can become very sore and inflamed if the dog has an allergic reaction. Preventive treatment is obviously essential, but if you suspect an allergic reaction, you may need to seek veterinary advice.

Food intolerance and environmental factors, such as dust mites or pollen, can also cause major skin problems. The problem here is finding the root cause, and this can only be done by a process of elimination, such as removing specific foods from the diet. Again, you will need help from your vet to deal with this issue.

Inherited conditions

Like all breeds, the Poodle does have some breed-related disorders. If your dog is diagnosed with any of the diseases listed here, it is important to remember that they can affect offspring, so it is not wise to breed affected dogs.

There are now recognized screening tests to enable breeders to check for affected individuals and hence reduce the prevalence of these diseases within the breed. DNA testing is also becoming more widely available, and as research into the different genetic diseases progresses, more DNA tests are being developed.

Addison's disease

Also known as hypoadrenocorticism, is caused by insufficient production of adrenal hormone by the adrenal gland. The signs include vomiting, diarrhea, lethargy, and poor appetite. In severe cases, heart function can be affected. Hormone replacement therapy will be needed for the duration of a dog's life. Standard Poodles are more likely to be affected.

Atrial septal defects

This is a relatively rare heart malformation where there is a hole between the upper chambers. A small hole will cause few problems, but symptoms associated with a larger hole include coughing, breathlessness, intolerance to exercise and, at its most severe, collapse. The hole can be repaired with surgery. Standard Poodles are more likely to be affected.

Chronic active hepatitis

This causes inflammation and tissue death in the liver, and is generally first seen in dogs around five to seven years of age. Signs include, vomiting, weight loss, diarrhea, lethargy, and increased water intake.The condition can be managed with medication.

Cushing's disease

Also known as hyperadrenocorticism, is caused by too much production of adrenal hormone by the adrenal gland. This is usually seen in older dogs, but can begin much earlier in life. Some of the more common signs are excessive appetite, drinking large amounts of water, frequent urination, large pot belly, thin skin, hair loss on the body, thinning of hair, and drastic change of hair texture.

Epilepsy

Epilepsy is a common cause of seizures in all varieties of Poodles. The form that typically affects Poodles generally is inherited, and it can result in either mild or severe seizures. Often, it can be controlled with medication.

Hip dysplasia

In dogs with this structural problem, the ball and socket joint of the hip develops incorrectly so that the head of the femur (ball) and the acetabulum of the pelvis (socket) do not fit snugly. This causes pain in the joint, and may be seen as lameness in dogs as young as five months old, with deterioration into severe arthritis over time. Gentle exercise, keeping the dog at a good weight, anti-inflammatory drugs, and home management are all part of the treatment. Severe cases may require surgery.

Poodles, like many other breeds, can be affected by hip dysplasia, and all potential breeding animls should therefore be screened by having their hips scored. X-rays are submitted to the Orthopedic Foundation for Animals or PennHIP, where they are graded according to the degree of hip laxity.

Hip dysplasia is thought to have a genetic component, but the mode of inheritance has not been established, since multiple genes are involved. Environmental factors, such as nutrition and rapid growth, may also play a role in its development.

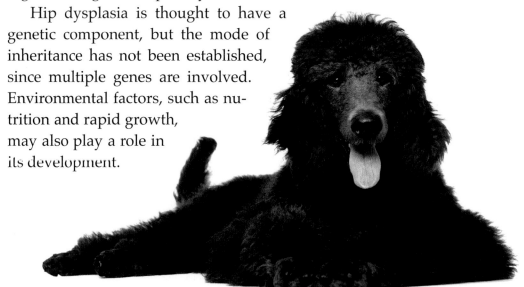

Hypothyroidism

Impaired thyroid gland function with low thyroid hormone levels, is seen in Poodles. It often develops slowly over several months or years. The dog may be listless, with a poor coat, and often gains weight. This disease is not easy to diagnose, and repeated testing may be necessary. It is treated with thyroid supplements.

Legge-Perthes disease

In this condition, the femoral head (ball) of the thighbone dies, resulting in severe pain and lameness. Early diagnosis, treatment through pain relief, and resting the affected back leg in a sling may be effective. Otherwise, surgery will be required.

Miniature Poodle dwarfism

This is a form of arthritis that affects skeletal development, growth, and maintenance of cartilage and bone. In addition to stunted growth, affected dogs often exhibit misshapen limbs, shortened and bent long bones, enlarged joints, extended hind limbs, and flattening of the rib cage. Research shows that some 10 percent of Miniature Poodles carry the mutation that causes this. DNA testing is available.

Neonatal encephalopathy with seizures

This is a fatal disease of the brain in newborn Standard Poodles. Affected pups are weak, uncoordinated, and mentally dull from birth. If they survive the first few days, seizures develop, and the puppies die or are euthanized before they reach weaning age. A DNA test is now available that allows breeders to avoid producing affected puppies.

Optic nerve hypoplasia

This inherited eye disease, affecting Miniatures and Toys, is present from birth. The optic nerve fails to develop and, as a result, the pupil does not respond to light, resulting in blindness in the affected eye.

Patellar luxation

This is an orthopedic problem where the dog's kneecap slips out of place because of anatomical deformities in the joint. Treatment involves rest and anti-inflammatory medications. In more severe cases, surgery may be the best option. The Orthopedic Foundation for Animals (OFA) grades the degree of luxation or certifies that a dog is clear, based on X-rays.

Progressive retinal atrophy

This occurs in all three varieties but is more commonly seen in Toys and Miniatures. It is a condition which involves the destruction of the photoreceptors in the retina. As the disease progresses the retina shrivels up resulting in total loss of vision.

The onset of PRA can be between two and eight years of age. All breeding stock should be screened for this condition.

Sebaceous adenitis

This is a common disorder in Standard Poodles involving inflammation of sebaceous glands that normally lubricate the skin and hair follicles. Heredity plays a role, although the mode of inheritance is not yet understood. SA also has been reported in Miniature and Toy Poodles. Symptoms include scaling, flaking, and thickening of the skin, hair loss, and sometimes odor and sores caused by secondary infection.

Although there is no cure for SA, oil baths and other treatments often can keep symptoms under control.

Summing up

This has been a long list of health problems, but it was not my intention to scare you. Acquiring some basic knowledge is an asset, as it will allow you to spot signs of trouble at an early stage. Early diagnosis very often leads to the most effective treatment.

The Poodle as a breed is a generally healthy, energetic dog with a zest for life, and annual check-ups will be all she needs. As a companion, she will bring many happy memories in the years you will spend together.

Find Out More

Books

Bradshaw, John. *Dog Sense: How the New Science of Dog Behavior Can Make You a Better Friend to Your Pet*. New York: Basic Books, 2014.

Canova, Ali, Joe Canova, and Diane Godspeed, *Agility Training for You and Your Dog: From Backyard Fun to High-Performance Training*. New York: Lyons Press, 2008.

Eldredge, Debra, DVM, and Kate Eldredge, *Idiot's Guides: Dog Tricks*. New York: Alpha, 2015.

Eldredge, Debra M., DVM, Liisa D. Carlson, DVM, Delbert G. Carlson, DVM, and James M. Giffin, MD. *Dog Owner's Home Veterinary Handbook*. 4th Ed. New York: Howell Book House, 2007.

Stilwell, Victoria. *Train Your Dog Positively: Understand Your Dog and Solve Common Behavior Problems Including Separation Anxiety, Excessive Barking, Aggression, Housetraining, Leash Pulling, and More!* Ten Speed Press, 2013.

Websites

www.akc.org American Kennel Club

www.petmd.com PetMD

www.poodleclubofamerica.org Poodle Club of America

www.ukcdogs.com United Kennel Club

www. vipoodle.org Versatility in Poodles

agility in this case, a canine sport in which dogs navigate an obstacle course

breed standard a detailed written description of the ideal type, size, shape, colors, movement, and temperament of a dog breed

conforms aligns with, agrees with

docked cut or shortened

dysplasia a structural problem with the joints, when the bones do not fit properly together

heatstroke a medical condition in which the body overheats to a dangerous degree

muzzle (n) the nose and mouth of a dog; (v) to place a restraint on the mouth of a dog

neuter to make a male dog unable to create puppies

parasites organisms that live and feed on a host organism

pedigree the formal record of an animal's descent, usually showing it to be purebred

socialization the process of introducing a dog to as many different sights, sounds, animals, people and experiences as possible, so he will feel comfortable with them all

spay to make a female dog unable to create puppies

temperament the basic nature of an animal, especially as it affects their behavior

Index